Cistercian Studies Series: Number Sixty-Seven

BENEDICTUS

Cistercian Studies Series: Number Sixty-seven

BENEDICTUS

STUDIES IN HONOR
OF
ST BENEDICT OF NURSIA

Edited by E. Rozanne Elder

Cistercian Publications
Kalamazoo, Michigan
1981

Available in Britain and Europe through

A. R. Mowbray & Co Ltd
St Thomas House   Becket Street
Oxford   OX1 1SJ

To monks, nuns, and
scholars who have kept
alive the Benedictine tradition

Table of Contents

Preface

Fuit vir vitae venerabilis gratia et nomine Benedictus....
There was a man of venerable life, by grace and by name Blessed....

So begins the Life of St Benedict written by Gregory the Great
in his *Dialogues,* Book Two. And so begins the first antiphon for
the Feast of St Benedict, 21 March. Whether Pope St Gregory invent-
ed, exaggerated, or faithfully reported the events of his saint's
life is a question which scholars must debate and decide. St Benedict's matchless importance to western civilization lies not in his
deeds, but in the monastic Rule which bears his name. For a millen-
ium and a half, men and women have sought holiness by following his
'little rule for beginners'.

In celebration of the fifteen-hundredth anniversary of the birth
of St Benedict in 480, the monastic world sponsored numerous conferences, symposia, and special gatherings. As its mite, the Institute
of Cistercian Studies at Western Michigan University arranged special
sessions on the benedictine heritage as part of the Fifteenth Annual
International Medieval Studies Congress in May 1980. The participants
alone testify to the catholicity of the benedictine tradition: American, Canadian, British, and European scholars from the disciplines
of history--economic, social, constitutional, intellectual--,theology,
art history, liturgy, paleography, literature, and music rubbed should-
ers with monks and nuns, 'Black' and 'White', from the Roman Catholic,
the Anglican, and the Lutheran communions.

We have been able to publish here only a handful of the papers
presented during these very full three days, but we hope they give
some hint of the diversity of offerings. We should like to express
our special thanks to

-- Father Jean Leclercq, who, although prevented from joining the
     Kalamazoo celebration, has shared with us a paper he read
     elsewhere during the year;
--Professor Susan Millinger of Roanoke College, who organized a
     special session on Benedictine Monastic Founders at which
     two papers in this volume were presented;
--Professor Robert L. Shafer of the Asian Studies Committee of
     Western Michigan University, who organized the Eastern half
     of a series of sessions on comparative spirituality;
--The community of St Gregory's Abbey, Three Rivers, Michigan who
     treated conference participants to a buffet supper at their
     monastery and shared with them a festal Latin Vespers in
     honor of St Benedict;
--The staff of the Medieval Institute of Western Michigan Univer-
     sity, who accomplished, as they do each year, an impressive
     logistical feat in transporting, settling, and stimulating

more than a thousand Congress participants;

--Joanna Medioli, whose poster for the Congress celebrates St Benedict's birthday and has been used as cover art for this volume;

--The many scholars who make their way to Kalamazoo to share their
research and their enthusiasm for the Middle Ages, and this
year most especially to those who study and who live the monastic life according to the Rule of the man by grace and by
name Benedictus.

E. R. E.

THE MIRACLES OF SAINT BENEDICT

Benedicta Ward SLG

'One day when the brethren of this monastery were quarreling,
one of them met St Benedict outside the door and the saint immediately gave him this command: "Go and tell the brethren that they give
me no rest. I am leaving this house and let them know that I shall
not return until I bring from Aquitaine a man who shall be after my
own heart."'[1] The place is the abbey of St Benoît-sur-Loire at
Fleury; the man from Aquitaine Odo of Cluny, the reforming abbot
called in to deal with that turbulent house; and when the monk met
St Benedict in the cloister, the father of monasticism had been dead
for about four hundred years. It is a story with many layers of interest, and one which provides an entrance into the later tradition
about St Benedict of Nursia. Here there is a monastery being refound-
ed in France after the Norse invasions, a rough, undisciplined group
who, as the writer says, 'had been scattered far and wide through
fear of the enemy,' and were 'now united in body but divided in heart.
The turbulence of society is reflected in the cloister and the level
of comprehension of the monks is further illustrated by the fact that
when they were told that St Benedict had left them, 'they did not have
recourse to prayers and tears...but getting on their horses they rode
hither and thither to find him and bring him back by force.' John of
Salerno, the writer of this life of Odo of Cluny, scorns such a literal reaction; he is a monk of the spiritualizing tradition of Gregory the Great himself, and he tells the story as a vivid image of the
place of St Benedict as the peace-maker within the community of monks,
'those who choose the narrow way...so that not living by their own
will and obeying their own desires and passions, but walking by anoth-
ers judgement and orders, they dwell in monasteries and desire to have
an abbot over them.'[2] But the reaction of the monks was not by any
means unusual in tenth century Europe; the location of the saints was
taken very literally indeed, and the relationship men made with them
differed little if at all from their human relationships. If a great
lord withdrew his patronage, it was only reasonable to go and force
him to return to his duties if you could.

But what was St Benedict, the father of monks, the *advocatus
monachorum* to do with Fleury anyway? What has Odo of Cluny to say
in the matter? Why start so far away from St Benedict's own monastery in Italy, when he himself seems to have left it so rarely?
Cluny, Fleury, Monte Cassino: one of the links between them is undoubtedly the miracles of St Benedict, that tradition of signs and
wonders which is there in the first account by Saint Gregory the
Great and continues for many centuries elsewhere. I propose to examine briefly some miracles connected with the name of St Benedict

in order to see what insight can be gained from such material.
First of all there are the miracles of St Benedict which are related by St Gregory in the second book of the *Dialogues*. These claim
to be miracles connected with the life of St Benedict; they are presented as his *res gesta*, what St Benedict did when he was alive. Now
there are two aspects for comment here about such an account. The
first is the purpose of the account; it was specifically written for
the edification and encouragement of the reader; the second is that
it is not a biography but a hagiography. These are stories which
above all link the saint with the scriptural tradition of sanctity;
the miracles validate St Benedict, they place him in the main stream
of christian witness: 'I will tell you about the miracles of the
venerable man Benedict, *in praise of the Redeemer*.'[3] So we find that
St Benedict brings water from the rock, like Moses; he makes iron
float like Elisha; he causes Marus to walk on the water like St Peter;
ravens who feed him recall the feeding of Elijah in the wilderness;
like David, he grieves at the death of an enemy. He possesses, comments Peter, the interlocutor in the *Dialogues*, 'the spirit of all
the just'; but St Gregory as the narrator corrects him, 'Benedict'
he says 'possessed the spirit of one man only, the Saviour, who fills
the hearts of the faithful.'[4] Such miracles are related for a specific purpose; they are not the accidental deeds of a good man, they
are the miracles of a saint. They link him with the wonders God
showed through his predecessors, as an authentic saint of God, and
above all, as St Gregory says, they give to his life the only test
of christian sanctity, the likeness to Christ.
The miracles of St Benedict in the *Dialogues* of St Gregory can
be discussed in many ways, but this hagiographical dimension is fun-
damental to them. They are not primarily intended as an account of
the actions of the man Benedict (though that is not to say that they
weren't). They are about holiness of life in a christian context.
They are, for instance, about man restored to his right relationship
in control of the natural world--a broken dish mended, a man walking
on water, a thunderstorm obedient to a woman's prayers. They are
about insight so profound that it pierces the clouds that divide men
from one another, so that they are known for what they are, and a
servant cannot be mistaken for a king, nor can Exhilaratus take even
a sip of wine undetected. It is about that understanding of the vision of God that sees the whole of creation in a ray of the sun. And
it is about the battle with the demons, a fight so central to the
monastic life that it becomes visible in images and sounds: the demons shout and rage, they even sit on a stone to prevent it from form-
ing part of the house of God; like a dragon coiled round the monastery, the devil lay outside the walls, and the sight of him was shock
treatment enough for any monk who turned away in discouragement.
I do not wish to be misunderstood here. I am not saying that
these stories are literary fictions of no consequence. I mean that

the truth they embody and are designed to convey are more subtle and
important than a simplistic reading of the narrative suggests. The
images used to denote Christian sanctity are loaded with resonance
and meaning and they are equally at the disposal of writer, of ob-
servers, and of the saints themselves. This is not an easy point
to make clear but it has something to do with the fact that one ap-
prehends realities through the images at ones disposal and not otherwise. We need a way of perceiving in order to see, and especially
we need a way of writing in order to convey our understanding. To
say that an image is a type, that it is there in similar stories,
that it is found in previous accounts, does not mean that it can be
dismissed, as if we had found out the writer in the act of copying
from his neighbour in class; the resonances, the previous meaning,
the allusion, is precisely what the writer wishes us to discover.
The images are a lens, a telescope through which we view reality in
its long perspective. For instance when the death of St Benedict is
described in terms of light, brightness, and a road towards the east,
this echoes not only his own vision of 'the whole world gathered in
a single ray of light,'[5] it also contains all the echoes of heaven
in the Scriptures, and most of all the stories of the resurrection
of Christ, as it is meant to do. This man, they tell us, is dead
and alive unto God in Christ: 'the tomb of Christ who is risen, the
glory of Jesus' resurrection' still exists as the gate and entrance
into heaven and the images tell us far more than any amount of argument can.

   St Gregory presents St Benedict as the *vir dei*, the man of God
before all else. It is an ideal of holiness set in a scriptural
pattern and it is presented for edification: imitation of virtues,
not amazement at wonders is Gregory's purpose. The miracles of St
Benedict are the climax of St Gregory's description of the true
christian man, whose virtues have made him so like Christ that the
wonders and signs of the life of the new Adam flow again in the world
through his life and actions.

   Later, the second book of the *Dialogues* became in itself one of
the great patterns for accounts of sanctity. Again and again in the
Middle Ages saints' lives are modelled on either the *Life of St Benedict*, or the *Life of St Antony*, or the *Life of St Martin*. They become authenticating patterns, just as they themselves found authenti-
cation in the scriptures. For instance, when St Anselm strikes water from
the rock at Liberi, his biographer has in mind not only Moses but
also St Benedict;[6] when iron floats at Monte Cassino, the reference
is to both Elijah and to St Benedict.[7] Odo of Cluny delivered from
an accident at sea, recalls to his biographer 'what Peter and Paul
and then our father Benedict had previously merited.'[8] The curious
habit of receiving food from birds afflicted not only Elijah and Benedict but their successors, such as Cuthbert of Lindisfarne. The first
account of St Benedict then is no simple record of events, but a highly

sophisticated piece of theological writing.

But what became of this image of St Benedict in later accounts of him, above all in stories told after his death? For the Middle Ages had no doubt that a saint continues his work after his death; he is in fact more alive unto God and therefore more powerful and more accessible to men. The long tradition of northern Europe centres on the graves of the dead, on their relics, their dead bodies. Devotion in the early Middle Ages north of the Mediterranean could be called almost exclusively a thaumaturgy of the dead. Now the dead have one advantage over the living which gives them at once a popularity which is unique: they are dead, and they cannot answer back. If you consult a Simon Stylites, or an Antony, or a Macarius, you encounter a living person, whose replies are his own and not shaped by your predilections. You say, 'Father, speak a word to me' and you may be disconcerned, to say the least, by a reply listing your most private and secret faults and suggesting some practical remedies: 'Poemen said to Isaac, "Let go of a small part of your righteousness and in a few days you will be at peace."[9] 'Blessed Symeon said to Batacos, "for what reasons have you come here?" Batacos said, "I hope to transact business and bow before the feet of your holiness." "Wretched man," replied Symeon, "you don't mention that you are really here to act against Gelasios the man of God; go and ask to pardon at once."'[10]

St Benedict himself had not always in his lifetime been a comfort to his petitioners: 'he warned them to curb their sharp tongues and added that he would have them excommunicated if they did not.'[11] But go to the tomb of a dead saint and you have a quite different kind of freedom. You shape your requests, and by and large you hear the reply that your mind and imagination suggests to you. The stories of the posthumous miracles of the saints may reflect some aspects of the original tradition created around the living man, but ninety-nine percent of the time they reflect nothing of the kind. They are the reflection of an age, the record of the needs, sorrows, ambitions and ideals of each generation, each person, who experiences the contact with the dead. As such these collected stories of the miracles of the saints provide historical material of an unparalleled value. It is not the part of a historian, of course, to assess the supernatural value or content of such tales; but what he has to accept is the value given to them by medieval men and the vital role they actually played in their world. Once that is said, there are in these records glimpses of that person who is so rarely heard of as to be virtually unknown and inaudible, the medieval man in the street, or rather, the medieval monk in his cloister, since it was the monks who were the guardians of the relics and the recorders of the miracles. One does not expect to find out anything at all about St Benedict from such records; but one can see in a bewildering kaleidoscope of material what generation after generation made of him.

Let us look at two such records. First there are the *Miracles of St Benedict*, written under that title by Desiderius, abbot of Monte Cassino, in the second half of the eleventh century in Italy at St Benedict's own monastery. The account is in three books, and in form it follows the pattern of the *Dialogues* of St Gregory; there is an interlocutor, Theophilus in place of Peter, who encourages the discourse with his questions and comments. The intention of the writer is similar to that of St Gregory: to show the action of God among contemporaries for the encouragement of faith.[12] As well as the similarity in form and intention between the two accounts, there are close parallels between the content and even the phrases. The second book of the *Dialogues* provided an exemplar for the work by Desiderius, thus creating a continuity between the early tradition and the later one. But the content is very different when taken as a whole. Few of the stories turn out to be about St Benedict at all: there are far more instances of supernatural rewards and punishments meted out to monks and their neighbours. The monastic practices of fasting, obedience, humility, simplicity, stability, are rewarded; demons are rebuked; and enemies of the monastery receive severe and dramatic punishments for their crimes. In two cases only are there accounts of men cured of illness at the tomb of St Benedict: a boy visiting the abbey with his father is cured of insanity by lying all night before the altar of St Benedict;[13] the nephew of a monk of the house, Theoderic, was paralyzed and cured after praying before the altar of St Benedict and also having had the relics of St Maur placed on his chest.[14] The stories recorded in the last book by Desiderius hardly concern either St Benedict or the monastery, but are set in Rome and are connected with the reforms of Pope Gregory VII. What can be discovered from this account, then, is first, the interest in the tradition of St Benedict by an eleventh century abbot and his desire to show that St Benedict's protection and power are still at work in his monastery; secondly, a shift in interest from St Benedict as the father of monks to St Benedict as the protector of his own monastery at Monte Cassino; thirdly, a curious lack of miracles actually performed by St Benedict in connection with the tomb where St Gregory says he was buried. This is not a collection of posthumous shrine miracles in any ordinary sense of the term, and perhaps this was because the claim of Monte Cassino to exclusive rights in the body of St Benedict had been challenged.

This brings us at once to a very difficult question indeed: where is the body of St Benedict? Monte Cassino assumed that St Benedict was buried there, as St Gregory says, and that he either never went away or if he did at least some of him returned. But the abbey of Fleury claimed, and still claims with startling perseverance, that they once stole the body of the saint and took it to France and kept it there. It is still a debatable question. For the purpose of this paper, it is what each side said and claimed

that matters—not, note, what each side really believed, because it
would be a mistake to think medieval men, least of all monks, were
deceived by their own reasoning. To summarize the rival claims:
the body of St Benedict was said to have been stolen from its sepulchre at Monte Cassino by the monk Aigulf sent by Mummoldus, second
abbot of Fleury, at the end of the eighth century. Desiderius does
not allude to this, either to deny or admit it, nor does he use a
quotation from the *Dialogues* of St Gregory which would have fitted
the case: 'the holy martyrs can perform outstanding miracles where
their bodies rest; but...in places where their bodies do not actually lie buried,...they must perform still greater miracles.'[15]   The
theft is, however, mentioned in Paul the Deacon's *History of the
Lombards;* and it forms the basis of the *History of the Translation*
by Adrevald of Fleury. It was necessary at Fleury to emphasize the
point that these were really the relics of St Benedict, and throughout the Fleury collection this recurrs: in the story of the translation, the first book by Adrevald, there is a story about *quidam*
"someone", who warned the pope in a dream that the relics were being
stolen from Italy.[16] The legal question of the ownership of the relics is mentioned in two chapters of Adrevald's first book of miracles,
where he describes a request from the pope for their return; Fleury
is represented as having no counter-claim, and therefore being ready
to surrender the body. Adrevald says it was St Benedict himself who
refused to go back—he came to Fleury *propria sponte* and will not
leave it unless he chooses to do so.[17] Another vision recorded by
Andrew of Fleury at the end of the eleventh century continues the
theme of the favour of St Benedict towards Fleury, but here it is
also said that St Benedict shares his favours equally with Fleury
and Monte Cassino: Richard, abbot of Monte Cassino, is said to have
had a vision of St Benedict assuring him that this was so.[18]

    The account written by Adrevald is an instance of a theme fam-
iliar in the ninth and tenth centuries of *pius furtus*. Adrevald
had to show that the relics taken to Fleury where genuine; this
meant that he had to show equally clearly that they were stolen.
Phrases like 'by divine revelation' or 'St Benedict wills it' are
the only justification for keeping what was taken; there is no attempt to show that the relics were in any way the legal property of
Fleury. To have the body was all important, and the next most important thing was to show that it worked. It was genuine because
it was really taken from its original shrine, and Monte Cassino was
shown to admit this even in its counter-claims. It was also genuine
because it worked miracles. The remainder of the books of miracles
of St Benedict at Fleury are the assertion of just this claim; where
the miracle collection is, there is the body—at Fleury and not at
Monte Cassino.

    At Fleury the tradition of the miracles of St Benedict under-
went a further change. The book of miracles of St Benedict at

Fleury covers two and a half centuries and comes from the hands of
five different writers, each with his own style, interests, and
background. They reflect changes in culture, secular as well as
monastic, to an amazing degree and, not surprisingly, they say virtually nothing about St Benedict.

The possible qualification to this is that there was an in-
direct concern at Fleury to present a continuation with the tradition of the miracles of St Benedict as recorded in the *Dialogues* of
St Gregory. In the abbey church at Fleury there are carvings on
some of the pillars from the twelfth century and earlier. They show
scenes from the miracles of St Benedict as recorded by St Gregory:
St Benedict fed by a raven, tempted by a **devil**, holding his Rule,
and finally shown giving his blessing to the family of the carver,
the monk Hugh de St Marie, who was also the writer of the last book
of miracles. It is an amazing piece of propaganda by which the
standard, authentic miracles of St Benedict are transferred visual-
ly to Fleury. Over the lintel of a door a scene is carved of the
translation of the relics and the first cures at the shrine, a suggestion of continuity which is permanent and vivid and beyond argument.

Another visual aid at the abbey shows another side of the change
in location perhaps even more radically. The carvings say, St Benedict is here; there is an unbroken tradition from his life until this
moment and this place. In the excavations under the high altar the
first place where the shrine of the supposed relics was placed has
been uncovered. Around it, facing towards it, are stone sarcophagi
of the ninth century containing the bodies of local magnates, determined to be as close as possible to this great friend of God at the
resurrection, when they were certain to need all the help they could
get. This practical concern with *Dies illa, dies ira* led these men,
who, if the miracle-books are to be believed, were no great friends
of the abbey during their lives, to take this final step to secure
the saint's intercession in the next world:

> 'what shall I, frail man, be pleading,
> who for me be interceeding
> when the just are mercy needing?'

The coffins provide a very firm statement about the position St
Benedict had come to hold in the countryside of the Loire.

St Benedict is seen, therefore, as the intercessor for Fleury
and its dependants. The carvings and the coffins tell the same story
and the miracles fill in the details. Each writer presents St Benedict in different situations but in each story the image has a remarkable consistancy: he is now no longer the father of monks, the abbot
of a monastery, but the lord of his domains, the patron of a house
and its inmates, responsible for them, as they are **also** responsible

to him. The stories contain a wealth of detail therefore about monks
and lay people living near the abbey, and their relationship to it.
In the first book of miracles, for instance, written by Adrevald about
878/9, soon after the translation of the relics, the overwhelming im-
pression is of a violent society, of small knights at war with one
another, to whom the possessions of the abbey are fair game in a con-
tinual struggle for land and loot. In seven instances, the stories
show the anger of St Benedict falling upon those who attacked the
monastery, in four instances his protection is extended towards its
inmates. What is interesting for the historian is to trace the dynam-
ics of power, the aggression and defence pattern in this small part
of tenth-century Europe. What is the significance of this anger of
a saint? Who sees him as active and what does this mean in society?
When Rohan, count of Orleons, for instance, attacks the lands of
Fleury in a small piece of ground ajoining his own property, he is
acting according to obvious methods for obvious ends; what defense
does a monastery have? It needs to protect and consolidate lands
just as much as the count, and it has at its disposal a force more
potent than any army of knights: when the count falls ill, the abbey,
through the writer Adrevald who records the sequence of events, sees
the attack and the illness as cause and effect: St Benedict, he says,
has acted mysteriously to defend his own and punish aggressors.[19] The
relics of the saint are recognized as possessing mysterious but in-
calculable powers and in each incident where this supernatural sanc-
tion is asserted to have acted, the abbey is that much more secure.
Imagination can be a more forceful shield than swords. The most notable characteristic of St Benedict at Fleury is that he proves his
presence there by miracles; and the social situation in which the abbey exists determines that those miracles shall be above all acts of
power and ferocity. Adrevald explicitly compares the relationship
between St Benedict and Fleury with the covenant between Jehovah and
Israel in which devotion is repaid by protection and the destruction
of enemies. It was a covenant of mutual help and dependance, in
which the monks were by no means always submissive. The monk Christian, the sacristan, guarded the shrine of the saint with energy, and
when some treasures were stolen from it he confronted St Benedict
with displeasure: 'Believe me, father Benedict,' he said, 'if you
do not see to it that those bracelets are returned to me, I will never light another candle to you.'[20] A strange transformation for
Saint Benedict, 'beloved of the Lord.'
     After a long gap occasioned by the disturbances of the tenth
century and the Norse invasions, Aimon of Fleury wrote two more books
of the miracles of St Benedict. Odo of Cluny had taken control of
the abbey and under his successor, Abbo, Fleury knew sufficient security for monastic life and learning to emerge. Aimon was a child-
oblate, coming from a noble family in the Périgord, and he proved
to be an able writer. Beginning in 1000, he records instances of

miracles connected with the body of St Benedict at Fleury; again
there is the firm assertion that the saint is really there by the
proof of his miracles in that place. And what, beyond that central
fact, emerges in these stories? In nine instances punishment falls
upon the enemies of the abbey; the local knights have by no means
learned their lesson, nor have conditions become much more peaceable
than when Adrevald wrote; Fleury and its lands are still a focus for
hostility and attack, and the assertion of the power of St Benedict
must still be made. Rainald, Gerard of Limoges, Herbert of Sully,
Romuald of Chartres, pass through these pages, with their attempts
to acquire monastic property and the penalty this brings upon them.
The point the writer is making is that St Benedict is *tutor loci*,
the protector of that place, a violent saint with unlimited power
who will repay attacks on what is his by supernatural retribution.
Once the ills that happen to these men have been linked with their
inroads on the abbey lands, a powerful piece of propaganda is in
existence and it is at least meant as a deterrent. It needed only
a few instances of misfortunes to befall those who trespassed against
the abbey and its patron for the power of St Benedict to become an
established feature of social life in the valley of the Loire. Romuald, a citizen from Chartres, let his pigs root in the part of a
forest belonging to Fleury; he resisted the orders of the monks, even
appealed to the bishop of Orleans: it was not his fault that the
pigs had strayed. But he fell ill with a fever and was dead by day-
break. The monks were not slow to point to this as condemnation by
their saint: 'Lo,' they said, 'the decree of the most just Judge
has fallen upon him.'[21] So we find the name of St Benedict taken
up as a war-cry in local fights: when, for instance, Adhemar of
Chabannais fought with a friend of the abbey, Boso of Poitou, Boso's
men were quick to use the name of the saint: 'they shouted the name
of St Benedict to the heavens; the whole valley echoed with it and
the woods threw back the name Benedict.'[22] A woman who lived near
the abbey entertained a travelling knight who was ignorant of the
powers at her disposal, and when he stole one of her geese she could
rest assured in the protection of 'the most holy Benedict who has
jurisdiction over this whole countryside.' Needless to say, the
knight fell from his horse and sustained lasting injuries, which in
turn increased respect for the saint.[23] The monks themselves were
particularly alert to the responsibility St Benedict had for them,
and when one of them was insulted and called a fool he felt justly
aggrieved with his saint: 'Most holy Benedict, my lord, are you then
sound asleep that you let one of your sons be insulted thus?'[24]

St Benedict has become in the imagination of local society a
power to be reckoned with; a terror to the enemies of the abbey, a
strong protector of its monks. It is a further stage in the projec-
tion of local needs and values onto the saint. It is a development
from the original image of St Benedict at Fleury. There is, however,

another element in these stories of Aimon. As well as marauding
knights and cunning monks, there are pilgrims--men, women, and
children--who come to the shrine to pray to St Benedict and offer
gifts, rich gifts very often and eventually enough to rebuild the
church. The pilgrims are also presented in the stories as the
people of St Benedict; his protective power extends from his own
monks to them, and at times his power is displayed in curing their
diseases. Moreover, another element in these stories is significant:
St Benedict is not the only saint who works miracles now at Fleury;
at his side stands St Mary, the lady of Fleury, lending him her as-
sistance in at least half the miracles recorded by Aimon. It is a
common phenomenon of the times: St Mary moves into the centre of
medieval devotion from this time onwards, and eventually miracles
which were once attributed to the prayers of saints such as St Benedict were not only shared with her but transferred totally to her.
But here it is of particular interest for Fleury, since it is in
contrast to the early exclusive claim that St Benedict alone worked
wonders there. Perhaps the suggestion is that his place at Fleury
is now well-established and no longer needs quite such exclusive
emphasis.

Aimon wished to continue this record but was deflected to writing the *Lives of the Abbots of Fleury*. The work of recording the
miracles of St Benedict was taken up by another monk of Fleury, Andrew. He began in 1043 and was still writing in 1056. He was the
son of a local noble family and entered Fleury under the abbot Gauze-
lin. The four books of miracles which he wrote are in a style notably more ornate than that of his predecessors, a symptom of the times
as well as a reflection of his own interests. Again, the preponder-
ance of miracles are those of vengeance: knights die suddenly after
pillaging the lands of the abbey; serfs become paralyzed when they
work on festivals; the serf Stabilis who ran away from the abbey
and lived as free man in the town for several years is summoned in
a dream by his lord, St Benedict, and returns to his former serfdom.[25]
Litigation over monastic property results in punishments by the saint
not only of the ones who bring the cases but for the lawyers involved
in opposition to the monks. St Benedict is still shown as having a
care for his own people, and for the pilgrims: in time of plague,
his relics are taken in procession over the countryside as a pledge
of his power to deliver his own. Several of the sick are reported
as receiving healing by prayer at his shrine. And the stories are
no longer confined to Fleury: St Benedict is now venerated in Spain
and Aquitaine, and pilgrims come from there to give thanks to him
at Fleury, thus continuing to focus veneration for St Benedict there.

The next writer to take up the tale of violence in high places
is the monk-poet Ralph of Tortaire, who was born in 1063 and became
a monk at Fleury. He recorded eighteen miracles of vengeance, thirteen instances of protection and favour, and three cures at the shrine.

Ralph is a lively and enterprising writer, and in his stories there
are instances of the power of the saint exercised against animals--
dogs, pigs, and peacocks. The increasing interest in miracles connected with the sacraments is illustrated here, too: a dying man
is miraculously enabled to recover sufficiently to make his confession, by prayer to St Benedict. Ralph feels compelled, as none of
his predecessors did, to explain the miracles of vengeance in theological terms: for our profit, for the chastisement of our souls,
for our eternal benefit, he says; not at all how the earlier writers thought about it. For them punishment had a more practical and
immediate value. But the old theme of St Benedict as a stern patron
is still prominent: in his first chapter, Ralph ascribes the death
of Eudes, the brother of King Henry, to his contempt for the possessions of the abbey.[26] The sick were still cured by the relics of
the saint, but equally those who attacked his lands or worked on
his feast day or molested his people were punished. Warinus, for
instance, a peasant on the lands of the abbey, was attacked by a
knight, Hugh Bidulf, and had his arm broken; he complained to St
Benedict before his shrine: 'My lord, St Benedict, I am your slave;
you are my lord. This arm which is broken then belongs to you. I
would not complain if you had broken it yourself, but why should
Hugh Bidulf be allowed to do it?'[27] Belinus, another servant of the
abbey, turned to the saint in illness saying, 'if foreigners can secure my lord's favour, how much more should he care for me, since
he is my lord according to law and they only come here from a far
country?'[28] The powers of St Benedict continue, then, into the eleven-
the century; what has changed is the increase in foreigners, pilgrims,
who now seem to have first claim on the saint, so that one of the
saint's own people has to remind himself that he also can appeal to
him.

The last miracles in the collection were recorded by the monk
of Hugh of St Mary, who added eleven miracles in 1118. The collection ends there, either from a break in the manuscript or in reality.
There is a marked difference in these stories from their predecessors:
apart from the first miracle, which is an account of the deliverance
of a captive, they are all cures of pilgrims. They happened at the
shrine, and are recorded in detail, with names, dates, diseases, and
the manner of the cure. One instance from Hugh's record will show
how similar these were to cures at other healing shrines and how different from the usual miracles of St Benedict which were best described thus: 'This punishment was deserved, since he had opposed
the friend of Christ with all the pride of his heart, and was laid
low because of his sin.'[29]

> A woman from the town, who was called Hosanna, on
> that same night [the feast of the Annunciation,
> 25 March 1114] lay prostrate before the altar,

holding out her arm and hand which were in need
of healing. For a grievous sickness had taken all
the strength from both and she could not even flex
her fingers. When she had prayed earnestly, she
found that she was cured and felt no pain at all.[30]

By 1118 the miracles of St Benedict had achieved their primary
purpose of focusing devotion to St Benedict on the place where his
body was buried at Fleury. How strong this centralization was can
be further illustrated by reference to the veneration of the monks
of Cluny for St Benedict. This was primarily focused on his shrine
at Fleury. Relations between Cluny and Monte Cassino were, in the
eleventh century, cordial: Hugh of Cluny visited Monte Cassino in
1083 and established a confraternity between the two abbeys,[31] Peter
Damian visited and admired the life at both monasteries.[32] But nevertheless, the veneration of the Cluniacs for St Benedict's relics was
focused on Fleury. The feast of the translation of the body of St
Benedict to Fleury was celebrated at Cluny in the eleventh century[33]
and Peter the Venerable supplied a new hymn for it in the twelfth,
acclaiming the wonders surrounding the body of the Italian saint in
his new shrine in Gaul:

> Claris coniubila Gallia cantibus
> Laetaris Benedicti patris ossibus
> Felix quae gremio condita proprio
> Servas membra celebria.
>
> Miris Italiae fulserat actibus
> Gallos irradiat corpore mortuus
> Signis ad tumuim crebrius emicat
> Illustrans patriam novam.[34]

The vital contact between the two monasteries had been made long
before, when Odo of Cluny became abbot of Fleury. John of Salerno
says, as we have seen, that Odo was called, elected, and pre-ordained
to be abbot of Fleury by St Benedict himself. During Odo's abbacy,
St Benedict appeared in visions, supporting his reforms, and he appeared also to Odo himself while he was keeping vigil at Fleury 'before the body of the saint.'[35] It also seems from this account of
St Odo that the body of St Benedict had been removed from Fleury
during the Norse invasions and was restored, amid miracles, at this
time. This complete acceptance of Fleury as the miracle-working
shrine of St Benedict containing his body by the monks of Cluny is a
strong indication of the triumph of the propanganda of Fleury through
the records of miracles there.

While these miracles do not add directly to our knowledge of
St Benedict, they hold up a mirror to an age with exceptional clarity.

They point perhaps towards another fact about the place of the saints in history. We have for some years been **demythologizers** of the saints; if their legends are found to be unrelated to the facts of an edifying life, we dismiss them from the kalendar and from consideration, even when they are such major figures as St **George** and St Christopher. But the tradition about St Benedict indicates something further for consideration: the stories told about a saint after his death can have a more creative role in the lives of others than any plain historical facts about **his** life. Of course, with St Benedict there is always the fact to be borne in mind that his major contribution to civilization is that unique document of the human spirit, *The Rule*. But in addition, the legends, miracles, and stories provide not a dead weight of fanciful but outdated tradition, but a record of a living current of human experience, continually alive and infinitely varied. The texture of life is as varied as we care to make it, and for the monk especially one strand in it can still be the deeds of St Benedict.

Centre for Mediaeval and Renaissance Studies
Oxford.

NOTES

1. John of Salerno, *Life of St Odo of Cluny, Bibliotheca Clunia-censis,* 51E-2A; ed. Marrier and Duchesne (Paris, 1618).
2. *Rule of St Benedict,* ch. 5; ed. Justin McCann (London, 1952).
3. St Gregory the Great, *Dialogues* Bk. 1, p. 70; ed. U. Moricca (Rome, 1934).
4. Ibid., Bk. 11, p. 93.
5. Ibid., Bk. 11, p. 129.
6. Eadmer, *Life of St Anselm* Bk. 11, cap. xxxi; ed. R. W. Southern (Oxford, 1962).
7. Desiderius, *Dialogi di Miraculis Sancti Benedicti,* Bk. II, cap. 6; ed. G. Schwartz and A. Hofmeister (*MGH* XXXII, 1934).
8. *Life of St Odo,* 48A.
9. *Sayings of the Desert Fathers,* trans. Benedicta Ward (Kalamazoo-Oxford, 1975) 157.
10. Ibid., p. 39.
11. *Dialogues,* Bk. 11, p. 109.
12. Desiderius' *Dialogi,* Prologue, p. 1117.
13. Ibid., p. 1134.
14. Ibid., p. 1135.
15. Gregory, *Dialogues,* Bk. II, p. 134.
16. *Les Miracles de S Benoit écrits par Adrewald, Aimon, André, Raoul Tortaire et Hugues de Sainte Marie,* Cap. 1, Histoire de la Translation de Saint Benoit, viii, pp. 28-9; ed. E de Certain (Paris, 1858).
17. Ibid., Bk. 1, cap. xvii, pp. 40-46.
18. Ibid., Bk. VII, cap. xv, pp. 273-4.
19. Ibid., Bk. 1, cap. xix, p. 46.
20. Ibid., Bk. 1, cap. xxv, pp. 56-60.
21. Ibid., Bk. 11, cap. viii, pp. 109-10.
22. Ibid., Bk. 111, cap. v, pp. 135-42.
23. Ibid., Bk. 11, cap. xiv, pp. 116-17.
24. Ibid., Bk. III, cap viii, pp. 148-50.
25. Ibid., bk. VI, cap ii, pp. 218-20.
26. Ibid., Bk. VIII, cap. i, pp. 277-78.
27. Ibid., Bk. VIII, cap. xlvi, pp. 353-54.
28. Ibid., Bk. VIII, cap. xxxix, pp. 342-44.
29. Ibid., Bk. IV, cap. iv, pp. 179.
30. Ibid., Bk. IX, cap. xi, pp. 370-71.
31. *Chronica Monasterii Casinensis, MGH SS* VII, p. 741.
32. Peter Damian, 'Sermon for the Vigil of St Benedict,' *PL.* 144.
33. Udalric, *Consuetudines Cluniacensis,* i, 34; *PL.* 149:637.
34. Peter the Venerable, *Letters;* ed. G. Constable, (Harvard, 1967), vol. i, p. 320.
35. *Life of St Odo,* p. 53 D and E.

THE USE OF ROMANS 8:15 IN THE
REGULA MAGISTRI AND *REGULA BENEDICTI*

Claude J. Peifer, OSB

In chapter eight of Romans St Paul describes the state of the Christian who has been justified through faith and baptism. He has received the Spirit of Christ, who dwells in him and confers on him the life of the risen Lord, freeing him from the power of the flesh, sin, and death. He is therefore an adopted child of God, having received a share in Christ's own sonship, so that, like Christ, he has God as his Father and can call upon him with the same intimacy which Christ himself employed in addressing his heavenly Father, i.e., by using the name *Abba*: 'You have received the spirit of adoptive sonship, in which we cry out, "Abba, Father!"' (Rom 8:15).

This passage is cited once in the *Rule of St Benedict* in a rather unusual context. In chapter two, *What Kind of Person the Abbot Should Be,* the author explains that the abbot of the monastery occupies the place of Christ in the community. His title, *Abbas*, is a title of Christ: the monk is to believe that the abbot represents Christ for him because he calls him by one of Christ's names, *Abba*, for, 'as the apostle says, you have received the spirit of adoptive sonship, in which we cry out, "Abba, Father."' The RB therefore understands the cry of Romans 8:15 as addressed by the monk to Christ, not to the Father.

This curious exegesis of the RB has always constituted a problem, as there seems to be little precedent (and perhaps even less justification) for such an interpretation of the 'Abba, Pater.' It is now generally recognized, however, that the RB is dependent upon the RM, which in fact quotes Romans 8:15 at this same place and understands it in the same way. Chapter two of the RB seems clearly dependent upon chapter two of the RM, although it omits several passages of the Master's text and inserts several additions of its own. The first ten verses, however, are nearly identical in the two rules. In the citation of Romans 8:15 St Benedict has made only two minor changes, both probably designed to bring it into conformity with the received Latin text of Scripture. In addition to omitting *sed*, he also omits the RM's *Domino* ('We cry *to the Lord:* Abba, Father'). While this eliminates the RM's added insistence on the christological direction of the *Abba, Pater,* it in no way changes the understanding of it.

The problem of the origin of this apparently eccentric interpretation of St Paul is merely moved back one step by the admission of the priority of the RM. If the RB derived it from the RM, from what source did the Master draw it?

I propose to discuss two aspects of the question: One, the

general pattern of thought in early Christianity against which this
interpretation should be viewed; and two, some earlier traces of a
similar understanding of Romans 8:15.

A. *THE FATHERHOOD OF CHRIST IN THE EARLY CHURCH*

Our two monastic rules come out of a background in which the
fatherhood of Christ was almost a commonplace. While for us the
idea of applying the title and attributes of the Father to Christ
may seem theologically eccentric, many of the Fathers considered it
quite normal and in fact saw it as contained, at least implicitly,
in the Scriptures.[1]

From the viewpoint of intertrinitarian relationships, of course,
Jesus can only be called *Son*. From the viewpoint of the *oikonomia,*
however, Jesus represents his Father to the world and accordingly can
be said to exercise the role of fatherhood on our behalf. Divine sonship is a theme that frequently appears in the New Testament: Paul
speaks of adoptive sonship and John regards the Christian as a child
of God because begotten of him. For both Paul and John, however, the
Christian is a child of God, not of Christ. Modern biblical scholars
generally do not admit that the idea of Christ as Father occurs in
the New Testament.[2]

Nevertheless, there are passages in Scripture from which the
fatherhood of Christ can be deduced. In the Gospels Jesus calls his
disciples 'children' (Mk 10:24, Jn 13:35, 21:5) and promises not to
leave them 'orphans' (Jn 14:18). Since the New Testament identifies
Jesus with the Messianic King foretold by Isaiah (see Mt 4:15-16), he
receives the titles which belong to that personnage, among which is
'Father of the world to come' (Is 9:6). These and other passages
were appropriated by the Fathers in support of their contention that
Christ is our Father.

This line of interpretation began very early: the witnesses to
it extend back at least to the middle of the second century. The
following may be cited from before the year 200. The *Epistula Apostolorum* presents the disciples saying to the risen Jesus, 'You are our
Father,' whereupon he commissions them to become fathers and teachers.[3]
In the *Acts of Justin Martyr,* one of his companions replies to their
interrogator, 'Christ is our true Father, and our faith in him is our
mother.'[4] The so-called *Second Letter of Clement of Rome* says of
Christ, 'As a Father he called us sons.'[5] Melito of Sardis gives him
the title 'Father insofar as he begets.'[6] Irenaeus says that Christ,
like Jacob, begot the twelve-pillared foundation of the Church and
raised up sons of God.[7]

Thereafter it was especially in the Alexandrian Fathers that the
theme of Christ's fatherhood was cultivated. For Clement, Christ
the *Pedagogos* shows the tender care of a father or mother for his disciples; they are called 'the Christ-begotten.'[8] We are not to call

anyone on earth 'father' (Mt 23:9) because our human progenitor is
not the real cause of our being; we must recognize 'him who is truly
our father, when we are reborn through water.'[9] Likewise Origen af-
firms that Christ is 'the Father of every soul, as Adam is the father
of all human beings.'[10] He generally understood the *paterfamilias*
of the Gospel parables to represent Christ rather than God the Father.[11] As Origen was the most influential figure in the early Church,
in spite of controversies about his orthodoxy, his exegesis can be
found everywhere and was notably influential in determining the
course of interpretation in the West. It is no surprise, then, that
the fatherhood of Christ became a traditional theme among the western
Fathers.[12]

The early Church cultivated an intense devotion to Christ, which
is found especially in popular piety, as reflected, for instance, in
the acts of the martyrs.[13] This led to the phenomenon of praying the
psalms to Christ,[14] and even addressing the Lord's Prayer to him. The
latter usage is found in the *Regula Magistri (Thema Pater)*. It is
not clear whether the RB also intends this interpretation, since it
omits the Master's extensive commentary, and its two brief references
to the Lord's Prayer (RB 7.20, 13.13-14) are not decisive. Both rules,
however, frequently understand the psalms as prayers to Christ.[15] The
fatherhood of Christ is one aspect of the broader phenomenon of devotion to Christ.

Monastic circles seem to have been particularly influential in
promoting devotion to Christ as Father. Monasticism grew out of the
devout groups of virgins and ascetics who were strongly influenced
by the spirituality of the martyrs, and it also underwent the influence of Origen. It is precisely these milieux in which the concept
of Christ's fatherhood flourished. A fourth century monastic witness
to it exists in a text of Evagrius of Pontus, a fervent Origenist.
In answer to some monks who had asked him for spiritual counsel, he
replied: 'It is more fitting for you to seek the fruits of charity
among yourselves, since divine charity possesses you as a result of
apatheia, and indeed sons do not provide riches for their fathers,
but fathers for their sons. Therefore, since you are fathers, imitate Christ your Father, and nourish us at the appointed time with
the barley loaves of instruction for the betterment of our lives.'[16]
This passage shows not only the use of the title 'Father' to designate
Christ, but also its extension to his human representative, the spiritual father among the monks. This is precisely the relationship between Christ and the abbot which is shared by the RM and the RB.

The background against which the thought of our two rules must
be understood, then, is the christocentric devotion of the early
Church and especially of the ancient monastic tradition which they
inherited. They exhibit the same warm and tender devotion to Christ
as God. The term *Dominus* usually means Christ, and *Deus* often refers
to him. Prayer is addressed to him, including the prayer of the

psalms, and he is heard speaking in the Scriptures.[17] In view of
this, it is not surprising to find Christ designated in chapter two
as father of the monks, and the abbot's role understood to be that
of derivative father, the one who 'takes Christ's place.' All this
is the issue of a long tradition.

B. THE CHRISTOLOGICAL INTERPRETATION OF ROMANS 8:15

On the other hand, the biblical justification for it is not at
all commonplace. Other monastic writers do not cite Romans 8:15 as
a proof text when they speak of Christ as Father, or treat of the
abbot's role. So far a search through the patristic literature has
revealed very little in the way of other examples of this exegesis.
Some thirty years ago Balthasar Fischer was able to shed a little
light upon the subject: he drew attention to a byzantine liturgical
text known only in a ninth century Syriac translation, but judged
by its editor, Anton Baumstark, to be very ancient.[18] In this text
a paraphrase of the *Nunc Dimittis* is conceived as being addressed
to the Infant Christ by Simeon, and it then continues: 'Deliver us,
O Lord, from our follies, and grant us pardon, and deliver us from
the shame of our sins, so that you may fill our hearts with your
Holy Spirit, and we may cry out to you: "**Father**, our Father! Make
us sons of your Father!"' Though we cannot establish the date, we
have here a certain example from the eastern Church of the application of the 'Abba, Father' of Romans 8:15 (or Galatians 4:6) to
Christ. Is this perhaps a unique surviving example of an exegesis
which may have been shared by a number of eastern Fathers?

Fischer is certainly correct in looking to Origen as the source
of this exegesis. The Alexandrian likewise treats the *Nunc Dimittis*
as a prayer to Christ.[19] Moreover, he also understands Romans 8:15
as referring to Christ, not indeed with explicit citation of 'Abba,
Father,' but by citing the 'spirit of sonship' in a context which
explicitly calls Christ our Father: 'They are brothers who possess
the charism of sonship and are under the one Father, Christ'[20]; and,
even more explicitly, 'Christ indeed can be called Father and Mother,
for he is the Father of those who have the spirit of sonship and
Mother of those who need milk and not solid food. For Christ, speaking in Paul, became Father of the Ephesians by revealing the mysteries of wisdom to them, and the Mother of the Corinthians by feeding
them with milk.'[21] It is true that Origen refers Christ's fatherhood to Ephesians rather than Romans, but he is nevertheless thinking
of Romans 8:15, for this is the only place in the New Testament where
the expression 'spirit of sonship' occurs.[22]

There is one other link in this very fragmentary chain, a passage
in the *Hundred Gnostic Chapters* of Diadochus of Photike, a fifth century Greek ascetical writer who died around the time of St Benedict's
birth.[23] Diadochus is speaking of the difficulty of maintaining

recollection of 'the Lord Jesus': when passion troubles the soul, he says, recollection becomes impossible, but when the soul is free from passion it can again be fixed upon this desirable 'meditation.'

> For then the soul possesses that very grace which medi-
> tates with her and cries out 'Lord Jesus,' just as a
> mother teaches her child to say 'father' by repeating
> it with him until, in place of all his childish babbling,
> she has developed in him the habit of calling distinctly
> upon his father, even in his sleep. This is why the
> Apostle says, 'Likewise the Spirit comes to the aid of
> our weakness, for we do not know how to pray as we ought,
> but the Spirit himself intercedes for us with inexpres-
> sible groanings' (Rom 8:26). Indeed, as we are children
> in regard to the perfection of the virtue of prayer, we
> have an absolute need of the Spirit's help so that all our
> thoughts may be penetrated and softened by his inexpress-
> ible sweetness, and so that in this way, with all our af-
> fection, we may be brought to the recollection and love
> of our God and Father. Thus we cry out in him, as the
> divine Paul says again, as he marks the rhythm for us to
> call unceasingly to God our Father, 'Abba, Father' (Rom
> 8:15).

It would appear that Diadochus is speaking of prayer to Christ throughout this passage, despite the use of the terms 'God' and 'Father,' for the entire chapter has to do with 'recollection of the Lord Jesus.' He refers to Paul's affirmation that without divine grace we cannot say, 'Jesus is Lord,' (1 Cor 12:3) and expands it to affirm that thinking about Jesus and calling upon him are also the work of the Spirit in us. The Spirit gently helps us from within, like a mother patiently teaching her child to say 'father.' It is perhaps this metaphor, and the similarity of thought involved, that leads him to the action of the indwelling Spirit described in Romans; and he seems to equate this with the case he has just been discussing. Thus the 'Abba, Father' of Romans is taken to be the equivalent of the 'Lord Jesus' of First Corinthians.

This is an interesting link in the chain of tradition that may have extended from Origen to the RB, but which is otherwise represented only in the RM and the liturgical text cited above. Diadochus is in the ascetical tradition of Origen, which he received chiefly through Evagrius. On the other hand, he appears to have had close contacts with the west: his little diocese in Epirus bordered on the territory of the western Church, and he may have known Latin. According to Victor of Vita, he was the teacher of the african bishop to whom Victor dedicated his *History of the Persecution*,[24] and his work seems to have had extensive influence upon Julian Pomerius,

an African who later, in Gaul, was the teacher of Caesarius of
Arles.[25] It has been theorized that Diadochus may have been captured by the Vandals during a raid on Epirus and taken to Carthage as
a prisoner.[26]

Might Diadochus be the connection through whom the Origenian
interpretation of Romans 8:15 came to the West and entered the monastic tradition which the RB inherited? Or did the author of the RM
spontaneously come to this understanding, as Origen had done long
before, without any knowledge of previous examples of such an exegesis? The evidence is not sufficient to authorize a judgment on
this point: we can cite only rare and widely separated examples of
this exegesis, which do not necessarily establish a firm and contin-
uous tradition. The fatherhood of Christ, however, which the exegesis is meant to support, is well rooted in a long and thoroughly
documented patristic tradition.

St Bede Abbey
Peru, Illinois

NOTES

1. The concept of the fatherhood of Christ has been studied by H. S. Mayer, *Benediktinisches Ordensrecht in der Beuroner Congregation* (Beuron: Archabbey, 1932) 2/1.88-97; B. Steidle 'Heilige Vaterschaft,' *Benediktinische Monatschrift* 14 (1932) 215-226; 'Abba Vater' *ibid.* 16 (1934) 89-101; O. Casel 'Bemerkungen zu einem Text der Regula sancti Benedicti,' *Studien und Mitteilungen aus der Geschichte des Benediktinerordens* 61 (1947) 5-11; B. Steidle, *The Rule of St Benedict* (Canon City: Holy Cross Abbey, 1967) 82-89.
2. The text of 1 Jn 2:28-29 constitutes a difficulty, but modern commentators usually explain it so as to exclude the fatherhood of Christ. Some of the Fathers, however, admitted this interpretation, notably Augustine, *In Epistolam Iohannis ad Parthos* 4, 3.
3. *Epistula Apostolorum* 41-42, Ethiopic version: translation in E. Hennecke, *New Testament Apocrypha* (London: Lutterworth, 1963) 11. 220-221.
4. Recension B, paragraph 4: text in H. Musurillo, *The Acts of the Christian Martyrs* (Oxford: Clarendon, 1972) 50-51.
5. *Epistula Secunda Clementis* 1, 4.
6. *Homilia Paschalis*, 9. While some have considered this passage modalistic, a convincing argument for the orthodoxy of Melito is presented by G. Racle 'À propos du Christ-Père dans l'Homélie Paschale de Méliton de Sardes' *Recherches de Science Religieuse* 50 (1962) 400-408.
7. *Adversus Haereses* 4, 21, 3; see also 4, 31, 2.
8. *Pedagogos* 1, 6; 3, 12.
9. *Stromata* 3, 12.
10. *Peri archon* 4, 3, 7.
11. *Commentarium in Matthaeum* 10, 15; 15, 28.
12. See, for example, Hilary, *Comment. in Matt.* 20, 5; Jerome, *Comment. in Matt.* 4, 25; Ambrose, *Epistula* 76, 4; Augustine, *Sermo* 87, 9; *Epistula* 187.
13. See K. Baus 'Das Gebet der Märtyrer,' *Trierer Theologische Zeitschrift* 62 (1953) 19-32.
14. See B. Fischer 'Le Christ dans les Psaumes: La dévotion aux Psaumes dans l'Église des Martyrs,' *La Maison-Dieu* 27 (1951) 86-113.
15. B. Fischer 'Die Psalmenfrömmigkeit der Regula S. Benedicti,' *Liturgie und Mönchtum* 4 (1949) 22-35, 5 (1950) 64-79.
16. *Epistula* 61: W. Frankenberg, *Evagrius Ponticus*, Abhandlungen der königlichen Gesellschaft der Wissenschaften zu Göttingen, Philol.-hist. Klasse, Neue Folge 13, 2 (Berlin, 1912) 611. The importance of this text was first recognized by M. Rothenhäusler 'Der Vatername Christi,' *Studien und Mitteilungen aus der Geschichte*

des Benediktinerordens 52 (1934) 178-179.

17. On the RB's concept of Christ, see A. Kemmer 'Christ in the Rule of St Benedict,' *Monastic Studies* 3 (1965) 87-98; A. de Vogüé 'The Fatherhood of Christ,' *ibid.* 5 (1968) 45-57; A. Borias '"Dominus" et "Deus" dans la Règle de saint Benoît,' *Revue Bénédictine* 79 (1969) 414-423; 'Christ and the Monk,' *Monastic Studies* 10 (1974) 97-129.

18. B. Fischer 'Zu Benedikts Interpretation von Röm 8, 15,' *Colligere Fragmenta: Festschrift Alban Dold* (Beuron: Kunstverlag, 1952) 124-126; see A. Baumstark 'Zwei syrisch erhaltene Festgebete des byzantinischen Ritus,' *Oriens Christianus* 36 (1939) 52-67.

19. *Homiliae in Lucam*, preserved in **Jerome's** translation in PL 26:268.

20. *Expositio in Proverbia* 6; PG 17:180. This appears to be an authentic work of Origen. It was edited by Cardinal Mai in the *Bibliotheca Nova Patrum* 7 (Rome, 1854) from Vatican codex 1802; Mai's edition is **reprinted** in PG 17:161-252.

21. *Ibid.* 20; PG 17:212.

22. The reference to Ephesians is undoubtedly due to the occurrence of the term 'sonship' in Eph 1:5: 'He [the Father] destined us in love unto sonship through Jesus Christ.' The term sonship otherwise occurs only in Rom 8:15, 23; 9:4; and Gal 4:5.

23. Chapter 61: É. de Places, *Diadoque de Photicé: Oeuvres spirituelles*, Sources Chrétiennes 5 bis (Paris: Éditions du Cerf, 1955) 120-121.

24. Victor of Vita, *Historia persecutionis Africanae provinciae*, Prologue: CSEL 7, 3.

25. *Julianus Pomerius, The Contemplative Life*, translated by M. J. Suelzer, Ancient Christian Writers 4 (Westminster: Newman, 1947).

26. H. Marrou 'Diadoque de Photiké et Victor de Vita,' *Revue des études anciennes* 45 (1943) 225-232. On what is known about Diadochus, see É. de Places, *Diadoque...*, **Introduction,** or *Dictionnaire de la Spiritualité* 3:817-834.

LOSS OF SELF IN THE DEGREES OF HUMILITY
IN THE RULE OF SAINT BENEDICT, CHAPTER VII

Thomas X. Davis, O.C.S.O.

The God-Exemplar

'In overflowing wrath for a moment I hid my face from you, but
with everlasting love I will have compassion on you, says the Lord.'[1]
In the christian dimension, the loss of self through the attitude of
humility has its ancient exemplar in the tender, compassionate, humble love of Yahweh for his people. Such an anthropomorphic revelation of **divinity** as this culminates in Jesus, the Son of God. Christ,
the Revelation of God, styles himself as 'the least' in the **kingdom**[2]
because his love is a *kenosis*, a giving up of self in the lowly death
on a cross.[3] Our God is a humble, **loving God.**

The Self and Its Dynamic

Our existence, the self, is a gift whereby we participate in
the life of this humble loving God.[4] With this existence comes the
divine command[5] to know oneself, and to develop from **an** unrealized
to a realized identification with the divine. Insight motivates
the self from an identification with lower animal impulses, a nar-
cissistic self, a selfish love, i.e., pride, vanity, passions, and
other ego-centric desires,[6] towards an identification with a personality formed by relationships **with** things, other persons, and God.
By the gradual purification of these relationships through sincere
love as taught in the Gospels, we discover a still greater self that
can experience the fruits of true, sincere love, namely, 'powerlessness' and 'nothingness.' An authentic love experience is one of to-
tal surrender to another; one gives all and holds nothing back. One's
identity will shift; it will no longer be formed by impulses or relationships but it will become an identity formed by union with God.

Union with God through the No-Self

Union with God is the beginning of an encounter we 'know **not**';
yet it is truly the place where our self belongs. We arrive here
by a ruthless campaign against all forms of illusion and the desires
that come from self-complacency and spiritual ambition. A total surrender of our life, a **holocaust,** leads to a discovery within our-
selves of a no-self: of deep silence, humble detachment before everything that exists, and before God. Even our prayer is not to be the
source of our identity; it can be a net ensnaring us in our own self-
regard.[7] Cassian teaches that prayer is not perfect if in it a monk

is aware of himself or of the words he is praying.[8]   This no-self
is monastic purity of heart.

Humility in the *Rule* of St Benedict

Chapter VII of the Rule of St Benedict 'Of Humility' in continuity with christian tradition views humility as a disposition basic
to integrating human and divine life: God comes to us, we go to
God through the *kenosis* of Christ.   The ladder spoken of in the
opening words of this chapter, 'a ladder set up by our ascending
actions like the one Jacob saw in his vision,'[9] is not then to be
taken as suggestive of a method or technique.   Rather, the ladder
symbolizes our life: resting on a humbled heart, it is raised to
heaven by the Lord himself.   In other words, a humbled personality
provides the disposition needed for removing any duplicity, any
complexity; it prepares the self for the manifestation and presence
of God.

The Twelve Degrees of Humility

The twelve degrees of humility are paradigmatic of very early
christian teaching on contemplative prayer as the no-self.   In order to see this connection, let us cite some examples from the early
fathers at each of the twelve degrees.
The seventeenth homily attributed to Macarius the Great[10] reveals the need to enter our darkened self and put to death the evil
serpent existing deep in the abyss of our soul at the root of our
thought.   Death, forgetfulness of God, comes from having this serpent digging itself ever deeper into the chambers of our life.   The
first degree of humility is to flee this forgetfulness by being always mindful of all that God commands and exposing every part of our
abyss to his divine presence.   Facing squarely a life based on this
forgetfulness within brings us a fear and dread of its consequences:
negligence, falsity, unfaithfulness here, eternal damnation hereafter.   This initial phase of fear and dread is not to be regarded
as something pertaining to primitive religion.   This fear is an initial means of understanding God's absolute sovereignty over self, a
basic experience of the self as 'nothing' in comparison with a Being
so totally other.   This brings about the realization that self-manip-
ulative control over one's life has to be broken through, if there
is to be any attempt to destroy or change the usual mode of living
and thinking, of choosing and willing, of awareness and consciousness.
Without this breakthrough there is no departure from the world of illusion.
The second degree of humility is 'that a person love not his own
will, seek not to fulfill his own desires but carry out in deed that
word of the Lord, "I came not to do my own will but to do the will of

him who sent me."'[11] This places selfishness opposite selflessness, that loss of self which comes from doing what must be done.[12]
The Holy Spirit of repentance, accompanying the experience of God's
sovereignty, makes us begin to exercise discernment about our life's
activities, with the result that the relationship between body and
soul is purified and healed. This discernment restores proper bal-
ance between body and soul and orientates the self towards its true
identity in the loss of self. The self becomes 'reasonable' in the
sense of very early desert spirituality:[13] that is, a person who
does what must be done under the influence of the Holy Spirit of God.

Obedience to any superior in imitation of Jesus, the Rule's
third degree of humility, integrates the loss of self into the tradition of paschal transfiguration. Such an obedience, by rooting
out addiction to desires stemming from the self, brings conscious
and unconscious mental activity to peace. It enables the self to
die to personal choice and brings the flexibility and readiness to
be at the disposal of God.

The real shift of the center of gravity from self to God, caus-
ing every component of the self to disappear before the divine, is
achieved by embracing patience with a quiet consciousness, *tacita
conscientia,* in all the hard, contrary, and even unjust dimensions
of life. This, humility's fourth degree, gives deep inner peace:
apatheia. It literally allows the self to be supplanted by the
sensitiveness of the Good Spirit of God, whose dwelling--the self
--needs to be a spacious place free of all anger and sadness, as
the *Shepherd of Hermas* teaches.[14]

Integral to patience with a quiet consciousness is a humble
manifestation of one's evil thoughts and past secret sins to the
abbot. This, for St Benedict, is the fifth degree of humility.
The faith experience and the experience of having a life-giving
father--the fruits of this degree--remove from self the deep ten-
dency to sin and darkness, illusion, **deception,** pretence, and vain-
glory--all of which intercept the workings of divine mercy and dis-
tort our relationships. This experience of faith and of a life-
giving merciful father ought not be underestimated in the destruction of selfishness.[15]

Since the self is clever in avoiding the recognition of illu-
sions, especially those cherished about **itself,** it is possible to
grow old in spiritual endeavor without really being humble in self-
knowledge. Instead of a gradual discovery of the no-self before
God, there emerges from such spiritual discipline a kind of subtle
presumption or delicate effrontery in our relationship to one another and to God. By contrast, in the sixth degree of humility, the
disciple is asked to be content[16] with what is poor and abject and
to see himself a sinful and useless laborer. Macarius' twenty-sixth
homily teaches that this attitude is the sign of an authentic
Christian.[17]

'Happy the person who thinks himself no better than dirt!'[18]
This beatitude of Evagrius is a joyful echo of the seventh degree
of humility: to believe with deep, intimate conviction, *intimo cre-
dat affectu,* that one is lower and more vile than anything else,
that one is a worm and not a man[19]...just poor mountain dirt![20]
Recognition of God comes in direct proportion to the depth of the
recesses of self that our inner humbleness can plumb. When the
self is without any desires, for the sake of the kingdom of God,
it is actually led by a desire so great that it can comprehend no
thing. The self becomes a no-self, for nothing can satisfy it save
the Divine Presence. No previously determined conditions and limi-
tations are given for this presence.[21] The paradox that no-self is
an incomprehensibly great desire means that you are not giving God
a name along with the rest of creation,[22] nor equating God with the
name given him and thereby making the divine after your own personal
image and likeness.

Responding to the Divine Presence as the principal formative
influence in our life is the eighth degree of humility: to do only
what the example of the seniors and the Rule authorizes. An authentic person cannot interpret his life apart from a wholeness reflected in and integrated by his spiritual and physical environment. For,
like a spiritual master, people and things place an unexplicable
burden on us and so enable us to know our own nothingness and our
need to give and receive, to love and be loved.

The ninth degree of humility is to maintain silence until
questioned. Talkativeness can be a subtle means of self-affirmation,
self-assertiveness, arrogance, and consequently an indication that
a person has not yet come to a proper self-knowledge and sincere
compunction. Intelligent silence, that is, an esteem for and correct use of speaking with emphasis on silence and listening, is the
matrix of authentic relationships with others and of contemplative
prayer.[23]

The growing awareness of our illusory and distorted self through
everything that hurts self-esteem reveals to us our inner repulsive-
ness, fragmentation, wounds. The temptation is to disguise or to
flee from these areas by flattery, ostentation, being easily and read-
ily moved to laughter or by a lack of seriousness.[24] Not to give in
to this urge to escape is the tenth degree of humility. This pain-
ful revelation is the beginning of *penthos*: an abiding and develop-
ing sense of separation of self from God. Weeping, the gift of tears,
heralds a growth in *apatheia,* that deep inner stillness and peace,
the loss of self before the Divine Presence.

The eleventh degree of humility: speaking with few and reasonable words, *pauca et rationabilia,* maintains the self as 'reasonable'
in very early desert spirituality.[25] But, in this instance, it guards
against levity of mind and ignorance. By a verbal and mental silence,
traces of self-will are dissipated and preparation is made to receive

with freedom that wisdom and Spirit which cannot be seen, heard, or conceived.[26]

The self's curiosity about things, persons, or events must be eliminated so that it does not turn to them to indulge in some dissolute or disordered passion, emotion, thought, or desire. It also needs to be purified of its mental images, concepts, ideas of God and of every dimension of its relationship with him. This purification produces attitudes and activities of harmony between the inner person and his outward conduct. They produce *hesychia, quies,* serenity, a tranquility of the inner and outer person proper to a **complete** renunciation of self in an absolute surrender to God. This manifestation of serenity and tranquility in our daily life, a transfiguration coming from the paschal mysteries, is the twelveth degree of humility. A humble quietness is revealed not only in the inner heart but also in the body.

Loss of Self Identified with Pure Prayer

Chapter VII of the Rule and Chapter XX, 'Of Reverence in Prayer,' have a remarkable similarity. In Chapter XX, purity of heart, humility, compunction, and tears are equated with the pure prayer, *oratio pura,* which brings salvation from God. The twelve degrees of Chapter VII see the same elements, purity of heart, humility, compunction, tears, as true selflessness or **loss** of self. The important conclusion is: pure prayer is identified with loss of self. In this identification, the Rule is consistent with the tradition of Evagrius and Cassian.[27]

The experience of selflessness is an experience of darkness, emptiness, nothingness. Because the self is a gift from God, a created participation in his life, this experience of darkness, emptiness, nothingness is likewise an experience of God working in us. *The Letter of Diognetus,* one of the earliest teachings on contemplative and mystic imitation of the powerlessness and long-suffering of God,[28] echos this in posing the question: Who really understood what God is before Jesus Christ came? Or, as Ignatius of Antioch expresses it in the circumstances of his own life: To be near the sword is to be near God.[29]

Love Casts Out Fear

The Rule of St Benedict makes available in its **teaching** of these twelve degrees the contemplative, mystic imitation of God. Fidelity to such an imitation of God and his Son, Jesus the Christ, brings one to that love which casts out fear. The Rule expresses this love by the Latin words *charitas Dei,* a phrase which carries the nuance that we identify with the divine love which is God, not that we love God in much the same way as we love another person.

The Man of the Spirit

The last sentence in Chapter VII of the Rule testifies that
these twelve degrees of selflessness are the working of the Holy
Spirit in us.[30] This presence of the Holy Spirit is in accord with
the Old and New Testaments. Scripture reveals that the outpouring
of the Spirit is the definitive sign that God has visited his people. The place proper for this Spirit is our emptiness, **nothingness,**
no-self.[31] He spans the incomprehensibility both of our void and
the total otherness of the divine. His presence means, first of all,
that the nothingness, the no-self, of an authentic love experience
proper to any complete surrender is far more total, radical and profound when given to God. Secondly, and here is the paradox, this
gift to God of being a no-self is **precisely** the ability to receive
the **gift** of being an authentic person, that is, one living with the
life--the Holy Spirit--of God. We imitate Jesus as revealed in the
Gospel of Mark: one who dies and gives up his spirit precisely because he was the Son of God.[32]

Abbey of New Clairvaux
Vina, California

NOTES

1. Is 54:8.
2. Mt 11:11.
3. Ph 2:1-12.
4. God is to the soul what the soul is to the body. This is a common patristic teaching.
5. This is the underlying theme of Mt 16:24-26 and other scriptural passages.
6. I.e., the illusory and/or empirical self.
7. Thomas Merton, *Mystics and Zen Masters* (New York: Farrar, Straus and Giroux, 1967) pp. 20 ff.
8. Cassian, *Conferences*, 9:31 ('The First Conference of Abbot Isaac').
9. *Rule of St Benedict*, Chapter VII.
10. Macarius the Great, *Homilies*, 17:15.
11. *Rule of St Benedict*, Chapter VII.
12. *Necessitas* is the word used in the second degree of humility.
13. See, for example, *The Letters of St Antony the Great*.
14. *Shepherd of Hermas*, Fifth Mandate I & II.
15. Cassian, *Conferences*, No. 18 ('The Conference of Abbot Piamun').
16. Lk 3:14.
17. Macarius the Great, *Homilies*, 26:11.
18. Evagrius Ponticus, *Chapters on Prayer*, No. 121.
19. Ps 21:7 (Vulgate); 22:6 (Hebrew).
20. *Life of Pachomius, Vita Prima Graeca*, No. 110.
21. Refer to the teaching of John of Lycopolis, Rufinus of Aquileia, *Historia Monachorum in Aegypto*, PL 21:395-8.
22. Gn 2:19-20.
23. Climacus, *Ladder*, Step 11.
24. *Apophthegmata, Alphabetical Collection*, John the Dwarf, No. 9; Poemen the Shepherd, No. 137.
25. *Letters of St Antony the Great; Letters of Ammonas*, Nos. 12 & 13.
26. 1 Cor 2:9 and teaching of John of Lycopolis, Rufinus of Aquileia, *Historia Monachorum in Aegypto*, PL 21:395-8.
27. Evagrius Ponticus, *Praktikos*, No. 23; Cassian, *Conferences*, 9:3.
28. *Letter to Diognetus*, No. 8 ff.
29. Ignatius of Antioch, *Letter to the Smyrnaeans*, No. 4.
30. *Rule of St Benedict*, Chapter VII.
31. Gn 1:2; Is 66:2.
32. Mk 15:39.

A DOCTRINE OF IGNORANCE:
THE ANNIHILATION OF INDIVIDUALITY
IN CHRISTIAN AND MUSLIM MYSTICISM

David N. Bell

That the nature of mystical experience and its interpretation is a complex and confusing problem has become clear in recent years. Few scholars nowadays would subscribe to the old and simple theory of the 'perennial philosophy' popularized by **Aldous** Huxley,[1] and recent developments in the study of mysticism have demonstrated clearly the very real difficulties of dealing with the intricate and important interaction of experience and interpretation. It is well-known now that there are major problems with R. C. Zaehner's analysis of mystical experience into panenhenic, monistic, and theistic[2], but the important critique of Zaehner's position put forth by Ninian Smart in 1965[3] has itself been seriously called into question. Smart's own position is that 'the monistic and theistic experiences are essentially similar; and that it is the correct *interpretation* of them which is at issue. The theist must maintain, in order to make sense of worship and devotion, that there is a distinction between the human individual and God. The non-theist, not being so concerned with devotion..., can more happily speak of identity with ultimate Reality, or can even dispense (as in Yoga and Theravāda Buddhism) with such a concept of the Absolute.'[4] In other words, 'the question of interpretation is the same as the question of God.'[5]

It may seem at first sight that Smart is here maintaining the same position as appears in the influential work of Walter Stace, namely, that all mystical experience is actually monistic and that only the interpretations differ,[6] but Smart specifically defends himself against this accusation. The thesis, he goes on, 'that maybe there is no essential distinction between what Zaehner has called monistic and theistic mysticism, does not at all entail that proponents of neo-Vedāntin views of a "perennial philosophy"...are right. The thesis "All introvertive mysticism is, as experience, essentially the same" does not entail any doctrine.'[7] The arguments of both Stace and Smart, however, necessarily assume that experience and interpretation can be meaningfully separated, but in a **number** of more recent articles we find it argued persuasively that this assumption may be quite incorrect. In the **view** of **Stephen** Katz, 'There are NO pure (i.e. unmediated) experiences....*all* experience is processed through, organized by, and makes itself available to us in extremely complex epistemological ways. The notion of unmediated experience seems, if not self-contradictory, at least empty.'[8] 'Belief,' he writes, 'shapes experience, just as experience shapes

belief.'[9] In this view he is followed by Peter Moore, who also as-
serts that 'there is a complex interplay between experience and doctrine, both at the external level where doctrine affects the description of an experience, and at the internal level where doctrine
may affect the substance of the experience itself. The suggestion
that the doctrinal elements in an account obscure the real nature
of the experience described makes about as much sense as saying that
if we want to know what a chicken really looks like we must first
pluck out all its feathers.'[10] The same idea, if not so neatly
expressed, may also be found in Robert Gimello[11] and Mircea Eliade.[12]
    Further difficulties arise from the nature of mystical writing
itself. The texts, as Carl Keller has demonstrated, 'do not necessarily reflect experience,'[13] and Ninian Smart himself has warned us
that we need to be on our guard in evaluating the mystics' reports.
'The existential impact and sacred context of the inner visions can
naturally lead to wider claims for them than the phenomenology might
warrant.'[14] And if it is true, as we are told *ad infinitum,* that
mystical experiences are actually extra-conceptual, then it follows
that any description can be at best only an approximation. The mystic must continually resort to figurative and allegorical language,
and there is every chance that a **particular** figure or allegory may
mean much more to the writer than it does to the reader. The only
alternative, of course, is to preserve a noble silence, and this
(with the exception of the Jewish writers[15]) the mystics seem unable
to do. The problem is epitomized by Po Chü-i's comment on Lao Tze:
'One who speaks does not know; one who knows is silent. These are
the words I hear from Lao Tze. If Lao Tze is really one who knows,
why did he write five thousand words?'[16]
    The source-material for the study of mystical experience, there-
fore, must be treated with great caution, and the investigator must
continually bear in mind first, that what a writer *says* may not be
an accurate reflection of the experience, and second, that even if
it is accurate, it may be a reflection of an experience which has
already been moulded by the metaphysical preconceptions of the writer's own doctrinal beliefs. We cannot, therefore, make any attempt
to examine the nature of mystical experience without being thoroughly
acquainted with the literary, philosophical, and theological traditions which form the writer's cultural background and which, consciously or unconsciously, must always affect his mental activities.
    Nor do our difficulties stop here. As I hope to demonstrate
in the following pages, there are still further problems to be taken
into account, and the question I will be concerned with is not so
much how far we can progress along a dangerous path strewn with bar-
riers and pit-falls, but whether we can even begin to make the attempt in the first place.
    The material I intend to consider is what the mystics of two
great theistic traditions--**Christianity** and Islām--have to say about

the annihilation of individuality and the absorption of this individuality in or by the being of God. The first thing which must
strike us most forcefully and obviously is that if the writers did
not deliberately qualify their accounts and descriptions, we could
come to no other conclusion but that at the height of mystical experience the soul and God become identical, one and the same thing,
with no distinction, division, or separation betweeen them. The
monastic writers of the twelfth century, for example, are not averse
to maintaining a total *(totus* or *omnimodus)* transformation of the
soul into God (we find it in Peter of Celle, Bernard of Clairvaux,
Gilbert of Hoyland, William of St Thierry, Aelred of Rievaulx, and
Henry of Clairvaux[17]), and in later christian writers--particularly
those of the Eckhartian tradition--the expressions are even more
extreme. 'If I am to know God **directly**,' says Eckhart, 'I must become completely He and He I: so that this He and this I become and
are one I.'[18] The spirit, says Ruysbroeck, 'receives the brightness which is God Himself...in the idle emptiness in which the
spirit has lost itself through fruitive love, and where it receives
without means the brightness of God, and is changed without inter-
ruption into that brightness which it receives.'[19] We are told by
his biographers that the **muslim** Abū'l-Ḥusayn al-Nūrī looked one
day at the Light, and did not cease from looking until he became
the Light.[20] According to Shihāb al-Dīn Suhrawardī Ḥalabī al-
Maqtūl, 'From the stage of "I" the seeker passes to the stage of
"I am not" and "Thou art," and then to the stage of "I am not and
Thou art not," for he is now himself one with the One.'[21] 'By union,' says Farīd al-Dīn ʿAṭṭār, 'I have been merged in the Unity,
I am become altogether apart from all else. I am Thou and Thou art
I--nay, not I, all is altogether Thou. I have passed away, "I" **and**
"Thou" no more exist. We have become one and I have become altogether Thou.'[22] And according to Muḥyī al-Dīn ibn ʿArabī, at the
height of mystical realization 'you and God are one and the same.'[23]
     There would be no difficulty in multiplying these examples,
but the point has been made. Such descriptions would lead us to
assume that the writers were maintaining the absolute identity of
God and the soul at the culmination of the mystical path, but if
we are to believe the writers themselves, such an assumption would
be heretical, blasphemous, and false. Your actions may be the actions of God, your attributes his attributes, your essence his essence, says ibn ʿArabī, 'but you do not thereby become He or He you
in either the greatest or the **least degree**.'[24] And for the christian writers, the whole tradition from Augustine onwards had specifically denied the **possibility** of the substantial identity of God
and the soul. It is clear from Augustine's comments that there
were some who thought it could be so, but that is not the opinion
of the Bishop of Hippo. 'If there are some who think that in the
future we will advance so far as to be changed into the substance

of God and thereby be made what He is, then they should take care
how they build up their ideas. I confess that I myself am not so
persuaded.'[25]

We may appreciate here the advantage offered by a favourite
analogy of the christian writers: that of water in wine, iron in
the fire, or air suffused with light.[26] The drop of water *seems*
to be wholly absorbed by the wine, the white-hot iron *seems* to become one with the fire, the air on a sunny day *seems* transformed
into sunlight, but *seems* is not the same as *is*. 'The iron does
not cease to be,' says Boehme, 'it is iron still: and the source
(or property) of the fire retains its own propriety: it does not
take the iron into it, but it penetrates (and shines) through the
iron; and it is iron then as well as before, free in itself: and
so also is the source or property of the fire. In such a manner
is the soul set in the Deity.'[27] But to what extent this explanation is simply an orthodox rationalization, a mere matter of words,
remains to be seen. Teresa of Avila, for example, whom few would
care to accuse of blasphemy and heresy, uses much more perilous
terminology. In the spiritual marriage, which is the highest state
possible for us here on earth, she tells us that the union of the
soul and God is like rain falling in a river: 'there is nothing but
water there and it is impossible to divide or separate the water
belonging to the river from that which fell from the heavens. Or
it is as if a tiny streamlet enters the sea, from which it will
find no way of separating itself, or as if in a room there were two
large windows through which the light streamed in: it enters in
different places but it all becomes one.'[28] How are we to reconcile
this with Augustinian orthodoxy? And what are the arguments used
by the christian and muslim writers to explain how, contrary to all
appearances, God remains ˉGod and the creature remains creature?

Of all the arguments they use, there are four which are of particular importance, and we may summarise them as follows: (1) the
argument of grace and nature; (2) the argument of participation;
(3) the argument of essence and attributes; and (4) the argument
of unity of will. As we shall see, these are not four separate and
discrete themes, but are to a considerable extent interrelated and
interdependent and, as we shall also see, the writers who make use
of these arguments are by no means agreed among themselves as to
precisely what the arguments are or how far they can be taken.

The argument from grace and nature is particularly common
among the christian writers, and is frequently supported by reference to Romans 8, 15 and 23, which refers to our adoption as sons
of God. Christ is one with God consubstantially, we are told, but
in our case, the sonship is by adoption. *'Non nati sed adoptati
sumus,'* says Rupert of Deutz, *'non natura sed adoptione.'*[29] It is
true that the Gospel of John promises that we and God shall be one
just as Christ and God are one, but it is a union *per gratiam* and

not *per naturam*.[30] We are told by William of St Thierry that man can
indeed be united to God by God and become one spirit *(unus spiritus)*
with him, but it is 'by the grace of the name and the effect of the
power,'[31] not by nature and by right. It is by derivation, says William, *ex derivatione*.[32] This explanation is a commonplace of the
mediaeval christian tradition, and examples of it are so frequent
as to make further references needless. What we must ask, however,
is to what extent it is a purely *terminological* explanation, a convenient use of technical expressions which cannot be verified experientially. In other words, if it is true that a mystic can experience that 'this He and this I become and are one I,' and if it is
also true (as we shall see) that the experience is extra-conceptual,
is there any way in which that mystic can also experience that this
apparent identity is not by nature, but by grace? We might well be
tempted to look upon this explanation with **grave suspicion**, and see
it as no more than a theological device to escape the peril of very
dangerous conclusions, but the situation is actually rather more complicated than appears at first sight. An examination of the texts
of those writers who use this explanation reveals quite clearly that
the distinction of union by grace and union by nature is intimately
linked with the doctrine of participation, and that what they are
actually saying is that union *per gratiam* or *ex derivatione* or *per
adoptionem* is a participated union in which the soul experiences
that God alone is the self-subsistent and that all the soul is or
has is entirely derived from him. We must turn, **therefore**, to a
brief consideration of the significance of participation in christian and muslim mysticism, and see whether this sheds any further
light on the question.

The Neo-Platonic doctrine of participation had a profound effect on both these traditions, and one of its great advantages, especially for the insistent monotheism of Islām, was in explaining
how we can posit the real existence of both God and human beings
without becoming straightforwardly dualistic. Ultimately, only
God exists in his own right, only he is self-subsistent, **only** he
has what the Buddhists would term *svabhāva* 'own-being.' All other
created things are what they are by participation in him and in his
attributes. 'There is no existence save his existence,' says ibn
ᶜArabī,[33] and the same principle may be found without difficulty in
a number of his followers.[34] It is not an idea, however, which is
restricted in any way to Islām, for according to Gregory of Nyssa,
whose debt to Platonism it is difficult to exaggerate, nothing
which can be apprehended by sense-perception or **contemplated** by
the understanding really exists. 'The transcendent essence and
cause of the universe on which **everything** depends, that alone exists. For even if the understanding looks upon any other existing
things, reason observes in absolutely **none** of them the self-suffi-
ciency by which they could exist without participating in true

Being.'[35] For the later Neo-Platonists and almost the whole of
the christian tradition both eastern and western, the being *(esse)*,
living *(vivere)*, sensing *(sentire)*, and rationality *(intelligere)*
of human beings are what they are only by participation in God.[36]
All our virtues are virtues only by participation: we are chaste,
says Augustine, by participation in chastity, wise by participation
in wisdom, good by participation in goodness, and so on.[37] All that
we are, in short, is *ex derivatione,* and it is this concept which
led Eckhart to those unfortunate extremes of expression for which
he was brought to trial. 'Every being and every single thing has
all its being, and all its unity, truth and goodness immediately
from God,'[38] and 'All creatures are pure nothing; there is no creature which is **anything.**'[39] But as Eckhart explains in his *Rechtfertigungsschrift,* he is not maintaining that things do not exist,
he is maintaining that for their existence they are wholly and completely dependent upon God. 'For if, without God, a creature has
any being, however small, then God is not the cause of all things.'[40]

If, however, we accept this framework, it is difficult to see
how we can meaningfully maintain that the soul and God are really
distinct. If there is truly no existence save his existence, and
if all of our being, life, **goodness,** consciousness, rationality,
sensing, is really God's being, life, goodness, and so on, how can
the soul know itself to be distinct from God when its very knowing
is ultimately God's knowing? William of St Thierry, for example,
can maintain that unity of spirit *(unitas spiritus)* is so called
'not only because the Holy Spirit effects it, or affects the spirit
of man to it, but because it is itself the Holy Spirit, God, Charity!'[41] By participation, it is true, but as far as the actual experience is concerned, can that qualifying phrase be any more than
a mere matter of words? Similarly, when ʿAbdul Karīm al-Jīlī, a
devoted adherent of the unity of being *(waḥdat al-wujūd),* tells us
that the true knowledge of God is the experiential realization 'that
you are He and He is you,' can we really believe him when he goes
on to qualify his statement by saying, 'The slave is slave and the
Lord is Lord. The slave does not become Lord, nor the Lord slave?'[42]

There are two main ways, neither of them particularly satis-
factory, in which the christian and muslim writers retain the distinction of the soul and God: firstly, by modifying the Neo-Platonic scheme by substituting creation for emanation; and secondly, by
limiting the extent to which the soul can realize its participation
in its Creator. In the first case, the writers submit that God
created finite things as participating in him, and that therefore,
as J. F. Anderson puts it, a finite object 'has *esse* without being
it.'[43] 'Since God is Supreme Being *(essentia),* that is, since He
is in the highest sense and is therefore immutable, so he gave being *(esse)* to the things which He created out of nothing, but not
being in the highest sense as He is. To some He gave more being

and to others less, and thus arranged these natures in a hierarchy
of being.'[44]   Created natures, therefore, are distinct from the Creator by definition, and with very few exceptions[45] and despite some
dubious terminology,[46] the christian writers never slide into the
heretical realms of emanationism.

The Muslims do not always appear quite so orthodox, and despite
the recognition by such as Shaykh Aḥmad Sirhindī of the very real
dangers of pantheism,[47] the concept of 'unity of being' proved extremely influential. In the system of ibn ʿArabī, *waḥdat al-wujūd*
does not, in fact, involve 'a substantial continuity between God
and creation,'[48] but there is no doubt that the idea was dangerous
and easily susceptible of misinterpretation. Furthermore, although
it may be true that in ibn ʿArabī's system God and his creation do
not form a single continuum, we must remember that what makes sense
philosophically may not make sense experientially. To combine the
concepts of creation and participation, in fact, is an extremely difficult task--Gilson simply calls it impossible[49]--and to say that
the soul is all that it is by participation in God, yet remains distinct from God because God created it that way, is not an especially
convincing reason as to why, when Jīlī says 'You are He and He is
you,' we should not take his words at face value.

The second explanation offered by our sources presents fewer
philosophical difficulties, but is associated with other problems
we have yet to consider. In this case, we are told that the soul's
participation in God is realized or actualized only to a certain
limited extent, and that however much the soul in drowned in the
ocean of Divinity,[50] it always retains something characteristic of
its own created self. This is an idea which leads us to the third
of the four arguments we are at present considering: the argument
of essence and attributes.

The principle here is simple: the writers distinguish the substance or essence of the soul from its accidents or attributes, and
maintain that it is only the latter which are assimilated into God
by participation and not the former. 'To lose yourself in a certain
way,' says Bernard of Clairvaux, 'as if you no longer existed; to be
totally unaware of yourself, emptied out from yourself, and virtually annihilated (*pene annullari*), is a divine experience, not a human
feeling.'[51] It is like a drop of water merged in wine, or iron in
the fire, or the air suffused with sunlight; all our human affections,
in a certain ineffable way, are melted and wholly poured into the will
of God. 'Otherwise, if something of man is left over in man, how will
God be all in all? The substance, no doubt, will remain (*manebit qui-
dem substantia*), but in another form, another glory, and another power.'[52] This same description in the same words also appears in Suso,[53]
and according to Ruysbroeck, no created being can pass away from its
own substance and become God. If it did, something would be added
to God's substance and that, says our author, is impossible.[54] The

principle is expressed very clearly in the *Conquista del Reino de Dios* of the remarkable Juan de los Ángeles: 'When I love God I cease not to be that which I am according to essence, but as touching the accidents. I say that the soul transformed in God through love lives more for God than for itself; for it desires and follows no longer that which the outer man craves, but that which God ordains. And as the soul lives rather where it loves than where it breathes, it follows that it belongs rather to the object of its love than to itself. And in this sense it may be said that the righteous are men in their accidents and gods in substance, since they live and are governed by the Divine Spirit of God: even as the iron that is red-hot remains iron although it be invested with the qualities of fire, appearing to be fire rather than iron in its essence, although in truth it is only so by participation, in the way wherein the righteous are gods.'[55] Sometimes, it is true, we come across dangerous terminology: William of St Thierry, for example, says that when we are made sons of God, the substance of God is not in any way changed, but our substance is transformed into something better *(nostra substantia in melius transmutatur)*.[56] But on the whole the Christians are content with this substance/accidents distinction. Among the Muslims, however, there is considerable disagreement. The formal, orthodox view appears in the important and well-known *Kashf al-Mahjūb* of Abu'l-Ḥasan al-Jullābī al-Hujwīrī, who explains that *fanā'* ('annihilation'[57]) does not mean the annihilation of essence, as some Sufis appear to think, but only the annihilation of the human attributes.[58] In this he is followed by a large number of later writers. The mystic 'passes away from his own attributes and persists in the attributes of God.'[59] But this is not the view of ʿAṭṭār. 'If you draw aside the veil from the Face of the Beloved,' he says, 'all that is hidden will be made manifest and you will become one with God, for then you will be *the very Essence* of the Divine.'[60] And this position is put with even greater clarity by ibn ʿArabī, Suhrawardī, Jīlī, and ʿAbdul Raḥmān Jāmī, all of whom state without any ambiguity that the actions, attributes, and essence of man become the actions, attributes, and essence of God.[61] 'He will see his essence to be the Essence of the One and his attributes to be the attributes of God and his actions to be the actions of God, because of his complete absorption in union with the Divine; and beyond this stage, there is no further stage of union for man.'[62] Yet Jīlī, as we have seen, still maintains the distinction between the slave and his Lord,[63] and ibn ʿArabī states categorically that you do not become God, nor does God become you 'in either the greatest or the least degree.'[64] Simply to state that God is always greater and always has priority, and that the soul which sinks into him *niemer grunt envindet,*[65] is of no real help, for our concern here is not whether the ocean and the stream are of the same size, but whether they are of the same

substance. If indeed there is a unity of being, and if the very
essence *(dhāt)* of the soul does become the essence of God, it is
difficult to see how there can be any awareness of a distinction
between the two. This is not to say that such a distinction does
not exist (for it is not the purpose of this paper to unravel the
secrets of the universe), but only that it is extremely difficult
to see how it could be experienced.

This distinction of actions, attributes, and essence is of direct relevance to the fourth and final argument we shall here consider, that of union of will, for according to Jīlī, it is when we
are illuminated by the divine actions that union of will is achieved.
'To one thus illumined it becomes plain that human agency is naught,
that he has no power or will of his own, and that all things are
done by the power of God who moves them and brings them to rest.'[66]
But beyond the actions lie the **attributes and the essence, and it is**
perfectly clear in the thought of Jīlī that unity of will is not
by any means the end of the mystical path. Among the christian writers, however, the situation is rather different, and there abound
a multitude of clear-cut statements which maintain categorically
that unity of will most certainly does mark the limit of our spiritual advancement. Bernard, for example, in a passage we have already cited, refers to the 'liquefying' of all human affections,
but speaks of their merging with the will of God, not with his essence,[67] and in the long discussion of the question in the seventy-
first sermon on the Song of Songs, he explains that when a soul is
said to be one spirit with God, this unity is brought about not by
confusion of natures, but by agreement of wills *(non confusio natur-
arum, sed voluntatum consensio)*.[68] Because God and man are not of
the same substance and nature, they cannot be said to be one *(unum)*;[69]
but if they adhere to each other by 'the glue of love,' they may truly be said to be one spirit. '**Yet** this unity is not brought about
by coherence of essences *(cohaerentia essentiarum)*, but by concur-
rence of wills *(conniventia voluntatum)*.'[70] This principle, that loss
of self is really the loss of self-will *(propria voluntas)*[71] and not
the ontological annihilation of the soul in God, occupies an established place in the christian tradition from an early date. It is
this, for example, which the *Rule of St Benedict* understands by loss
of self,[72] and the idea occurs again and again in later spiritual
writers. There are four knockers on the door which leads to union
with God, says Juan de los Ángeles, offering, petition, conformity
(conformarse), and union *(unirse)*, and in the last stage it is the
human will—no more than that—which is united with the Divine.[73]

It is clear, however, that not all the christian writers agree
with this. Luis de Granada, for **example,** an older contemporary of
Juan de los Ángeles, gives a clear description of unity of will and
recognizes it as being of immense importance, but as E. Allison Peers
points out, 'few, if any, who know the heights to **which** the greatest

Spanish mystics ascended, would claim for Fray Luís that this degree of union is **identical** with the summits of their lofty experience.'[74] Fray Luis is somewhat vague as to what lies beyond this
point, but there is certainly something there. Much more specific
information may be found in the work of the great Teresa: it is the
fifth mansions which are the Prayer of Union, and it is here that
we have 'a union with God's will of such a kind that no dissension
arises between the wills of God and the soul, but they are both
one.'[75] Yet there are **two** further mansions beyond this, the Spiritual Betrothal and the Spiritual Marriage,[76] and Teresa leaves us
in no doubt at all that unity of will is *not* the culmination of mystical ascent.

In the muslim writers, the situation is very **similar**. We have
already seen that for Jīlī it is illumination by the divine actions
which results in union of will, and that beyond this stage there is
illumination by the divine attributes and the divine essence. Shihāb
al-Dīn Suhrawardī (not Suhrawardī al-Maqtūl) also uses this scheme
and refers to the illumination of the divine actions as 'outer annihilation' *(fanā' al-ẓāhir)*, reserving the term 'inner annihilation'
(fanā' al-bāṭin) for the illumination by the divine attributes and
essence when 'the consciousness of the finite self is totally obli-
terated.'[77] Even the sober Junayd sees union of will only as a pre-
liminary to complete annihilation.[78] In other words, although there
is no doubt that union of will is of great significance for the mystical writers of both traditions, and although we do find it stated
that this is as far as **mortal** man can go, there is a considerable
amount of evidence that **this** last statement is simply not true. The
christian writers, like Luis of Granada, may be nervous about discussing the nature of the higher states, but this is far from saying
that they do not exist. One wonders, in fact, whether the great
figure of Abū Ḥāmid al-Ghazālī, who was accused of duplicity and a
double-standard, was not more honest than any we have considered so
far.

In the *Mishkāt al-Anwār*, Ghazālī considers the ecstatic utter-
ances *(shaṭaḥāt or shaṭḥīyāt)*[79] of Ḥusayn ibn Manṣūr al-Ḥallāj ('I
am the Real'; *Anā'l-Ḥaqq)*, Abū Yazīd al-Bisṭāmī ('Glory be to me!
How great is my glory!'; *Subḥānī! Mā a ʿẓamu sha'nī)*, and Abū Sā-
ʿid ibn Abī'l-Khayr ('There is nothing but God in my cloak'; *Mā'
fī'l-jubbati illā'llāh)*, and observes that in their experience
there was no plurality, that they could recollect nothing but God,
that they had no consciousness of self, and that their reason had
collapsed in a divine inebriation. But did they become God? No,
says Ghazālī, it is like looking at wine in a glass and mistaking
the former for the latter, 'but there is a difference between saying, 'The wine is the wine-glass,' and saying, 'It is *as if it were*
the wine-glass.'[80] In other words, according to our author, the
fanā' of Ḥallāj and the others led them into an erroneous inter-

pretation, and although it *seemed* that they had become God, this
was not in fact the case. Now this is a perfectly orthodox explanation (and defence) of these *shaṭaḥāt*, but it is what Ghazālī
goes on to add that is really significant: 'Beyond these truths
there are further mysteries which it is not permissible to investi-
gate' *(wa-warāʾa hādhihiʾl-ḥaqāʾiqi ayḍan asrārun lā yajūzuʾl-khawḍu
fī-hā)*.[81] In Zaehner's view (and using, for the moment his terminology) these 'further mysteries' were unquestionably monistic, and
Ghazālī the orthodox theist was little more than an outward show.[82]

That Ghazālī had a double standard is by no means a recent discovery: it was clearly recognised at an early date, and his admir-
er and critic, Abū Bakr ibn Ṭufayl, admitted that 'when addressing
himself to the general public [Ghazālī] "bound in one place and
loosed in another and denied certain things and then declared them
to be true"'.[83] There are certain opinions which a man keeps to
himself and which he only reveals to someone who himself holds it,[84]
and there is 'a secret knowledge which can be received only by the
gnostics in God, and ignored only by those who are heedless of
this.'[85] Ghazālī himself, he says, was quite mistaken on a number
of important points, but even ibn Ṭufayl found it necessary to con-
ceal certain matters with a light veil, although it was a veil which
could easily be withdrawn by those who were qualified to do so.[86]

This important distinction between public and private teaching
may perhaps lead the reader to suspect that I am drifting all too
close to maintaining the thesis of Stace, namely, that all mystical
experience is really monistic (and it is this which is taught to
the 'inner circle') and that fear of martyrdom, persecution, or
other administrative measures lead the mystic to interpret the experience in a more acceptable, exoteric, theistic fashion. This,
in fact, is not the case, and we may now move on to explain why it
is not.

The main point of my discussion so far has been to show that
the arguments adduced by the theistic writers as to why we should
not take their more extreme statements at face-value are not always
wholly persuasive. In some cases (particularly on the question of
whether the essence of the soul is annihilated in God and whether
union of will is the end of the path) there are major disagreements
among the various writers, and in other cases, what makes sense
philosophically (and also what does not: witness the unsuccessful
attempt at reconciling creation and participation) is hardly susceptible of experiential verification. Furthermore, all these arguments are dependent upon conceptual ideas--the conceptual distinction of grace and nature, for example, or of essence and attri-
butes--and according to all the mystical writers we have so far encountered, the highest mystical experience is extra-conceptual.
For the Christians, this was established by the authority of Augustine who classified all visionary experiences into three levels:

corporeal (by which he means the physical things we see with our
eyes), spiritual (by which he means all imaginary images and mental formations: these range from the most elementary acts of the
imagination to such complex visions as the Revelation of St John
the Divine), and intellectual (by which he means experiences which
are wholly beyond any mental constructions or conceptualizations
of any kind).[87] This scheme was adopted by the whole christian tradition, and it is the third level of vision--the extra-conceptual--
which pertains to the highest mystical experience. It is also the
idea behind Ghazālī's doctrine of *fanāʾal-fanāʾ*, the annihilation
of annihilation.

> When the worshipper thinks no longer of his worship or
> himself, but is altogether absorbed in Him Whom he wor-
> ships, that state, by the gnostics, is called the pas-
> sing away of mortality *(fanāʾ)*, when a man has so passed
> away from himself that he feels nothing of his bodily
> members, nor of what is passing without, nor what passes
> within his own mind. He is detached from all that and
> all that is detached from him: he is journeying first
> *to* his Lord, then at the end, *in* his Lord. But if during
> that state, the thought comes to him that he has passed
> away completely from himself, that is a blemish and a
> defilement. For perfect absorption means that he is un-
> conscious not only of himself, but of his absorption.
> For *fanāʾ* from *fanāʾ* is the goal of *fanāʾ*.[88]

The goal of the mystical path, therefore, is wholly beyond concepts
and, in consequence, wholly beyond description. It is also, therefore, wholly beyond any conceptual experience of pleasure or pain
('*Fanāʾ* is so complete,' says Sharafu'ddīn ʿUmār ibnu'l-Fāriḍ, 'that
not only do I feel no pleasure but my very essence *(dhāt)* has van-
ished'[89]), and in the words of ʿAbd al-Jabbār ibn al-Ḥusayn al-Niffarī, it is beyond letters, thoughts, and--most importantly--recol-
lection.[90] Recollection, says Niffarī, is a veil *(ḥijāb)*, for recollection demands concepts, and concepts are the veil of God.[91] Even
knowledge *(maʿrifa)* is a veil if we think we know,[92] just as for
Ghazālī *fanāʾ* is a concept and must itself be annihilated. Given
these premises, it follows that it is quite impossible to remember
(in the literal sense: 'to re-member, to build up again') the experience. We can remember *having had* it, just as we can remember having
had a deep and dreamless sleep when we wake up in the morning, but
we cannot remember *it*. This idea is well expressed in a passage
from the *De contemplando Deo* of William of St Thierry. The experience of God, he says, is beyond his understanding, and when he tries
to commit to memory its precise features *(lineamenta)* or to write
them down so that in the future he would be able to bring them back

again and have them at his command, the very fact and the experience force him to realize that what God says of the Spirit in the
gospel is true: You do not know whence he comes or whither he goes
(Jn 3:8).[93] We are in a realm which is empty of any concepts our
minds can grasp, a realm which is 'signless' (*animitta*, to use a
Buddhist term[94]), a realm which lacks any conceptual structures and
which, as a consequence, cannot be subjected to any descriptions,
even such descriptions as monistic and theistic. The concept of
fanā' must be annihilated in *fanā'al-fanā'*, but if *fanā'al-fanā'*
retains any meaning, it too must be annihilated.

There is still a further problem in that if what the mystics
say is correct, then not only are we in the absence of knowable
concepts, we are also in the absence of an individual knower. If
God truly takes over the soul and if all sense of 'I-ness' (*aniyya*)
is annihilated,[95] what is there left to do the remembering? If
God's existence is the only existence; if you lose all knowledge
and trace of your own existence;[96] if God is all in all and the soul
has no consciousness of itself,[97] then there remains nothing to do
the cognizing even if there remained concepts to be cognized! And
even if we maintain with Bernard that the soul's substance still
in some way remains distinct from God, it is difficult to see how
this can be of any practical consequence. All the attributes that
make an individual an individual--most **especially** his being, life,
and consciousness--are lost in God, and the situation is rather like
taking off your shoes when you go to bed at night. Your shoes will
still be waiting for you when you wake in the morning (whether you
believe they were there all night depends on whether you are a
thorough-going idealist or not), but when you were asleep, they
were to all intents and purposes totally **irrelevant**.[98]

What the mystics have done, therefore, is to preclude our saying anything at all about the nature of their highest experience,
and we may suspect that when they speak of it as a sleep (*somnium*)
or *stupor* or *soporatio* (which might mean unconsciousness) they may
be very close to the truth.[99] What we cannot say is that they were
all experiencing the same thing, and that this **'thing'** was either a
monistic identity or theistic communion with some Absolute Reality.
To state that two separate experiences are indescribable is not in
any way to suggest that they are identical; all that it means is
that the difference between them (if difference there be) is likewise
indescribable. If, then, there is nothing to be known conceptually
and no knower to know it; if there is nothing to be understood or
recollected or remembered, how much trust can we put in the asser-
tions that it is a personal God and not an impersonal Oneness which
is being encountered, that it is a matter of grace **and** not of nature, that it is a monistic and not theistic experience or vice-
versa? We are moving to a situation in which (if we may put it
thus) it is not so much a case of deciding how much interaction

there is between experience and interpretation, but of stating that
the experience, as it is relayed to us, is *entirely* interpretation.
As Gershom Scholem puts it, 'Because mystical experience as such is
formless, there is in principle no limit to the forms it can assume.'[100]
     This is why the ideas of Stace, and also those of Ninian Smart,
are logically suspect. We cannot say that all mystical experience is
monistic, or even that all mystical experiences are similar, because
there comes a stage at which knowledge of this type no longer has any
meaning. There is, as we have seen, plenty of evidence that at a certain point all sense of self-identity is lost and the human individual as such ceases to exist, but it is what happens at this point of
transition that defies our analyses. All too many scholars seem to
assume that the annihilation of the sense of self marks the end of
the mystical path, whereas it may actually be the first of its really
important stages. In the system of Plotinus, for example, it seems
fairly clear that loss of self is characteristic of two quite different levels, and that one of these levels is much superior to the other.
In the first case we have union with the Divine Mind *(nous chōristos)*,
when 'man becomes transformed into *nous*, when he through the *nous* sees
the *nous* and by that *nous* whom he sees when he becomes *nous*, he acquires
full and true self-knowledge. When I become that which is self-knowledge I know myself.'[101] It is a condition in which 'there is no difference between knower, object known, and the act of knowledge.'[102]
In the second case, however, which is union with the One, 'no *noēsis*
takes place, because the One is not intelligence but superior to it.'[103]
But to define conceptually and dualistically the experiential differ-
ences between two non-dualistic states is obviously beyond our capabil-
ities. The only people who really tried were the Buddhists, and to examine their contributions at the present time would take us too far
from our course.[104] If we may borrow the terminology of the Muslims,
fanā' 'annihilation' is followed by (or is coterminous with) *baqā'*
'subsistence,' but whereas we are not lacking sound evidence that
there are many who experienced *fanā'*, the nature of *baqā'* and the considerable disagreements which surround it are much more a matter of
philosophy and theology. Putting it another way, the mystical ascent may be likened to a flight of stairs which lead to a closed door.
We see the aspirant begin the path and see him climb the stairs; we
see him open the door and pass through, and then he is gone. We do
not know where he has gone; we do not know if there is anywhere to go;
we do not know if there was any 'he' to go anywhere at all. And if
we accept what the mystics themselves have told us, the aspirant himself may not know where he has gone or where he has been, and if he
comes back through the door, there is nothing he can say. He cannot
remember his journey and cannot describe it to us; he cannot say if
'he' went **anywhere**, for what happened to him is as incomprehensible
to himself as it is to us. As Richard of St Victor says, it is something above reason and beyond reason.[105]

I would suggest, therefore, that the only logical conclusion
we can come to is essentially a negative one. We can say that something is lost, but we cannot say what--if **anything**--is gained. The
ascent of the mystical path can certainly lead to an experience in
which all sense of self and all consciousness of human individuality is annihilated. Of that we can hardly be in doubt. But to go
one step beyond this and introduce monism, theism, *kaivalya*,[106] God,
Brahman, or anything else, brings us back immediately into the world
of theology, philosophy, concepts, beliefs, and opinions. At the moment of *fanā'*, the mystic, as we knew him, has gone, and where he
has gone is not susceptible to definition or description. To the
point of annihilation we can follow him as he can follow himself,
but beyond that the only doctrine we can meaningfully maintain is
surely a doctrine of ignorance.

Memorial University, Newfoundland

NOTES

1. See A. Huxley, *The Perennial Philosophy* (London, 1946). A very
    similar position is taken by Frithjof Schuon in *The Transcen-
    dental Unity of Religions* (New York, 1953).
2. See especially R. C. Zaehner, *Mysticism, Sacred and Profane* (Ox-
    ford, 1957). It is not my intention here to consider all the
    various criticisms of Zaehner's position, but much sound informa-
    tion and full bibliographical citations may be found in Steven
    T. Katz's useful article, 'Language, Epistemology, and Mysticism'
    in S. T. Katz, ed., *Mysticism and Philosophical Analysis* (= MPA)
    (London, 1978) 22–74.
3. See N. Smart, 'Interpretation and Mystical Experience' in *Religi-
    ous Studies* 1 (1965) 75–87. References to other important papers
    by Smart may be found in Katz's article cited in n. 2 above, MPA
    67, n. 8.
4. Smart, 'Interpretation,' 85–6.
5. *Ibid.*
6. See W. T. Stace, *Mysticism and Philosophy* (Philadelphia, 1960)
    and *The Teachings of the Mystics* (New York, 1960).
7. Smart, 'Interpretation,' 86.
8. Katz, 'Language, Epistemology...,' MPA 26.
9. *Ibid.* 30: see also page 59.
10. P. Moore, 'Mystical Experience, Mystical Doctrine, Mystical
    Technique,' MPA 110.
11. R. M. Gimello, 'Mysticism and Meditation,' MPA 175–176: 'This
    ...would require fully appreciating that interpretation can be
    actually ingredient in experience and need not be only something
    added to experience by the reflective intellect.' See also
    ibid., page 189.
12. See M. Eliade, *The Two and the One* (London, 1965) 77.
13. See C. A. Keller, 'Mystical Literature,' MPA 95.
14. N. Smart, 'Understanding Religious Experience,' MPA 14.
15. G. Scholem, in his *Major Trends in Jewish Mysticism* (New York,
    1954³) 15, observes that one of the distinguishing and unusual
    features of Jewish mysticism is 'the striking restraint observ-
    ed by the Kabbalists in referring to the supreme experience.'
    'The Kabbalists,' he continues, 'are no friends of mystical
    autobiography' (15). The recent compilation by Louis Jacobs,
    Jewish Mystical Testimonies (New York, 1977), simply confirms
    Scholem's observation.
16. The Chinese text and a different translation may be found in
    R. H. Blyth, *Zen in English Literature and Oriental Classics*
    (Tokyo, 1942) 141.
17. Illustrative examples from all these writers may be found in
    the article 'Divinisation' in the *Dictionnaire de spiritualité*
    (= DS) vol. 3, cols. 1399–1413. The list is not in the least

exhaustive (the article itself has major omissions: the Victor-
ines, English mystics, and Spanish mystics are conspicuous by
their absence), but it is quite **sufficient** for our present purposes.

18. G. Landauer, *Meister Eckharts Mystische Schriften* (Berlin, 1903)
    122, translated by Katz in MPA 41. For a different translation,
    see F. C. Happold, *Mysticism: A Study and an Anthology* (Penguin
    Books, 1970) 273.

19. *The Adornment of the Spiritual Marriage*, iii, translated by C.
    A. Wynschenk Dom and **reproduced** in Happold, *Mysticism*, 291.

20. This is reported by ʿAṭṭār in the *Tadhkirat al-Awliyāʾ* (ed. R.
    A. Nicholson; London/Leiden, 1905-7) 2:54, and Sarrāj in *Ki-
    tāb al-lumaʿ fiʾt-taṣawwuf* (ed. R. A. Nicholson; London/Leiden,
    1914) 40, 59.

21. Margaret Smith's translation in her *Readings from the Mystics of
    Islām* (London, 1950; rpt. 1972) 80.

22. *Ibid.* 90-91. 'When the paintings are hidden,' continues ʿAṭṭār,
    'thou wilt see the Painter. O brother, I will tell you the mys-
    tery of mysteries. Know, then, that painting and Painter are
    one!' (91).

23. *Ibid.* 101.

24. *Ibid.* 100. Suhrawardī al-Maqtūl, whose ideas we have cited at
    n. 21 above, also specifically denies that the soul can ever
    become God. See H. Corbin, *Oeuvres philosophiques et mystiques
    de Shihabaddin Yahya Sohrawardi* (Tehran/Paris, 1952) 1:228. Cp.
    also Jīlī's opinion cited at n. 42 below.

25. *De natura et gratia*, xxxiii, 37; PL 44:265. This opinion of
    Augustine is quoted with approval by Eriugena in his *De divisione
    naturae* V, 8; PL 122:877A-B, who adds further support from Boethi-
    us *(Liber de persona et duabus naturis*, vi; PL 64:1350C). Jerome,
    too, has no doubts on the matter: see his *Epistola* 133, 8; PL 22:
    1156.

26. For the history of this analogy and a survey of its use, see the
    excellent and comprehensive study by J. Pépin, 'Stilla aquae mo-
    dica multo infusa vino, ferrum ignitum, luce perfusus aer. 'L'or-
    igine de trois comparaisons familières à la théologie mystique
    médiévale,' in *Divinitas* 11 (1967) 331-375.

27. A somewhat modernized version of part of chapter 6 of *The Three-
    fold Life of Man* (London, 1909) 88, reproduced in E. Underhill,
    Mysticism (12th edn.; rpt. New York, 1972) 421. Cp. also n. 55
    below.

28. *The Interior Castle* VII, 2, 4, translated by E. A. Peers in his
    Saint Teresa of Jesus: The Complete Works (London/New York,
    1963) 2:335.

29. See **his** *De glorificatione Trinitatis* 2, 2 (PL 169:33C); 2, 13
    (PL 169:43D); *In evangelium sancti Joannis* 1 (PL 169:230A); 10
    (PL 169:629B). These texts, with others of similar importance

      may be found conveniently in DSp 3:1402.
30.   See, for example, the texts of Peter the Venerable, Arnold of
      Bonneval, Bernard of Clairvaux, Gilbert of Hoyland, William of
      St Thierry, and Isaac of Stella in DS 3:1402-1411.
31.   William of St Thierry, *Speculum fidei*; PL 180:394B (reading *ef-
      fectu virtutis* with M. M. Davy, ed., *Deux traités sur la foi*
      [Paris, 1959] 84, for PL 180:394B *affectu virtutis*). There is
      another English translation in *The Mirror of Faith*, Cistercian
      Fathers Series 15 (Cistercian Publications, Kalamazoo, Michigan)
      79.
32.   *Ibid.*
33.   See Smith, *Readings* 99. The statement and the idea are both well
      known. See A. E. Affifi, *The Mystical Philosophy of Muhyid Dīn-
      ibnul ʿArabī* (Cambridge, 1939) 1-24.
34.   Mahmūd al-Shabistarī clarifies and elaborates the ideas of ibn
      ʿArabī (see M. M. Sharif, ed., *A History of Muslim Philosophy*
      [Wiesbaden, 1963-66] 2:839-840), and the concept is taken about
      as far as it can go in the work of Jīlī (see R. A. Nicholson,
      Studies in Islāmic Mysticism [Cambridge, 1921] 77 ff.).
35.   Gregory of Nyssa, *De vita Moysis* II, 24-25; Sources chrétiennes
      (SCh) 1 ter:120; translated by A. J. Malherbe and E. Ferguson,
      Gregory of Nyssa: The Life of Moses (New York, 1978) 60.
36.   See P. Hadot, 'Etre, vie, pensée chez Plotin et avant Plotin,' in
      *Fondation Hardt, Entretiens sur l'antiquité classique: V, Les
      sources de Plotin* (Vandoeuvres-Genève, 1960) 105-157. In Augus-
      tine, see *De libero arbitrio* II, iii, 7; PL 32:1243-44; *De diver-
      sis quaestionibus* 83, 51, 1-2; PL 40:32; *Sermo* 43, 4; PL 38:255.
37.   See Augustine, *De Genesi ad litteram liber imperfectus* xvi, 57;
      PL 34:242; *De diversis quaestionibus* 83, 23; PL 40:16-17; *ibid.*
      51, 2; PL 40:32-33. The principle of participation is also cen-
      tral to the thought of Aquinas, the second most important forma-
      tive influence on the latin tradition. See especially L. B.
      Geiger, *La participation dans la philosophie de S. Thomas d'Aquin*
      (Paris, 1953) for an excellent, accurate, and comprehensive ac-
      count.
38.   **Proposition** VII, 7 in the *Rechtfertigungsschrift* translated by
      R. B. Blakney in his *Meister Eckhart* (New York, 1957) 278. See
      also Propositions I, 8 (262); I, 13 (262); II, 3 (263); III, 6
      (264); III, 7 (264); V, 1 (272); V, 8 (274); V, 13 (275); VI, 3
      (276); VII, 4 (277); VII, 6 (278); and IX, 36 (295).
39.   Proposition IX, 30; *ibid.* 294. See also **Propositions** IV, 15 (272);
      VIII, 15 (282); IX, 13 (286); IX, 43 (298); and IX, 46 (299).
40.   Proposition IX, 43 (298-299).
41.   *Epistola ad fratres de Monte-Dei* II, iii, 16; PL 184:349A (SCh 223:
      354; CF 12:95-96).
42.   See Sharif, ed., *A History*, 2:845. Jīlī himself, in fact, real-
      ized that there were problems with this: 'In reality there is

neither "slave" nor "Lord," since these are correlated terms.
When the "slave" is annulled, the "Lord" is necessarily annull-
ed, and nothing remains but God alone' (Nicholson, *Studies in
Islāmic Mysticism*, 128).

43. J. F. Anderson, *St Augustine and Being* (The Hague, 1965) 58.
44. Augustine, *De civitate Dei* XII, 2; PL 41:350. Aquinas provides
     a great deal of elaborate discussion of this theme.
45. See M. D. Chenu, *Nature, Man, and Society in the Twelfth Century*
     trans. by J. **Taylor** and L. K. Little (Chicago, 1968) 53-55.
46. Augustine, for example, speaks of the begetting of the Son as
     manatio in *De Trinitate* IV, xx, 27; PL 42:906-7, as does Eckhart
     (see Blakney, *Meister Eckhart*, 141).
47. See Sharif, *A History* 2:879-880: 'Pantheism was the real bane
     of Islām. The Mujaddid knew its fallacy and he was one of those
     who denounced it vehemently.'
48. A. Schimmel, *Mystical Dimensions of Islām* (Chapel Hill, 1975) 267.
49. E. Gilson, *The Christian Philosophy of St Augustine*, trans. L. E.
     M. Lynch (New York, 1967) 202: 'In short, Augustine undertook an
     undoubtedly impossible task, namely that of explaining creation
     in terms of participation.'
50. This is a very common Sufi metaphor. For some examples, see
     Smith, *Readings* 35, 55, 84, 86, 88, 110. The orthodox Abū'l-
     Mawāhib al-Shādhilī, however, makes it clear (though not especi-
     ally intelligible) that although you may be immersed 'in the sea
     of unity,' you must also 'stand upon the shore with all individual
     (see E. J. Jurjī, *Illumination in Islamic Mysticism* [Princeton,
     1938] 30, which is a **translation** of Shādhilī's *Qawānīn Ḥikam al-
     Ishrāq*).
51. *De diligendo Deo* x, 27; PL 182:990C (J. Leclercq *et al.*, *Sancti
     Bernardi Opera* [SBOp] [Rome, 1957-] 3:142; trans. CF 13:119).
52. *Ibid.* x, 28; PL 182:991B (SBOp 3:143; CF 13:120). Cp. Blosius'
     discussion reproduced in C. Butler, *Western Mysticism* (London,
     1967[3]) 9-10. The greek patristic tradition is particularly
     clear on this point, but to introduce greek examples would be
     to **increase** dramatically the number of references, and one has
     to stop somewhere.
53. See H. Suso, *Little Book of Eternal Wisdom and Little Book of
     Truth*, trans. J. M. Clark (London, 1953) 185. The passage is
     reproduced in Zaehner, *Mysticism, Sacred and Profane* 21; Under-
     hill, *Mysticism* 424; and a number of other places.
54. The relevant text from C. A. W. Dom's translation of *The Adorn-
     ment of the Spiritual Marriage* may be found reproduced in MPA 61.
55. E. A. Peers' translation in his *Studies of the Spanish Mystics*
     (London, 1951[2]) 1:302-303.
56. *Aenigma fidei;* PL 180:424B (see DS 3:1409; CF 9:86). Cp. also
     William's *Expositio in Cantica Canticorum;* PL 180:513C (DS 3:
     1409; SCh 82:252; CF 6:93): whatever enters the cellar of wine

becomes changed into wine 'because the fire of the love of God wholly *(totus)* assumes and consumes it, and, as happens with natural fire, **converts** it into its own substance' *(in suam convertit substantiam)*.

7. *Fanā⁾* is a term of very rich and wide meaning in Sufism and can be used in a whole variety of ways. See Schimmel, *Mystical Dimensions*, 130–148, for a very useful discussion. For two excellent collections of definitions and descriptions of *fanā⁾*, see A. J. Arberry, trans., *The Doctrine of the Ṣūfīs* (Cambridge, 1935; rpt. 1977) 120–132, and Jurji, *Illumination*, 70–73.

8. See Hujwīrī, *The Kashf al-Maḥjūb, The Oldest Persian Treatise on Sufism*, trans. R. A. Nicholson, (London, 1911; rp. 1959) 28, 243. Despite Hujwīrī's authority, few would agree with the comment in the *Shorter Encyclopaedia of Islām* (Ithaca, N.Y., 1965) 98 s.v. *fanā⁾*, that 'al-Hudjwīrī gives all the explanation that could be desired of *fanā⁾*.'

9. See Arberry, *The Doctrine* 121. As Junayd puts it, 'the attributes of the Beloved replace the **attributes** of the lover' (see Sarrāj, *Kitāb al-lumaᶜ*, 59.

0. Smith, *Readings*, 90.

1. For ibn ᶜArabī, see *ibid.* 100; for Suhrawardī, see Sharif, **ed.**, *A History* 1:367–368; for Jīlī, see Nicholson, *Studies in Islāmic Mysticism* 125–130 (Jīlī also discusses illumination by the Divine Names, but we need not consider that here and it does not affect our argument); and for Jāmī, see n. 62.

2. Smith, *Readings*, 125.

3. See n. 42 above.

4. See n. 24 **above.**

5. F. Pfeiffer, ed., *Meister Eckhart* (Leipzig, 1857) 501.

6. Nicholson, *Studies in Islāmic Mysticism*, 126.

7. See at nn. 51–52 **above.**

8. *In Cantica, sermo* (= SC) 71, 7; PL 183:1124C (SBOp 2:219). This passage is to be found in only two of the manuscripts, but the textual problems need not concern us here. The same idea, as stated at n. 70, is to be found in all manuscripts.

9. SC 71, 7; PL 183:1124B (SBOp 2:218). Bernard is here following Augustine, *De Trinitate* VI, iii, 4; PL 42:926. Cp. also Peter Lombard, *Sententiae* I, xxxi, 9; PL 192:606.

0. SC 71, 8; PL 183:1125B (SBOp 2:220).

1. This is an extremely important concept which we obviously cannot deal with in detail here. For a very sound account of the principles involved, see E. Gilson, *The Mystical Theology of Saint Bernard*, trans. A. H. C. Downes, (London, 1940) 55–59.

2. For a list of the relevant passages in the *Rule*, see the 'Concordance verbale' in A. de Vogüé's edition of *La Regle de saint Benoît* (SCh 182; Paris, 1972) 856, s.v. *voluntas*. See also T. X. Davis, 'Loss of Self in the Degrees of Humility in the Rule of St **Benedict,**

Chapter 7' in this volume.
73. See Peers, *Studies of the Spanish Mystics* 1:294-295.
74. *Ibid.* 46.
75. *Conceptions of the Love of God* iii, in Peers, *Complete Works of St
     Teresa* 2:377, and *Studies* 1:143.
76. See n. 28 above, and Peers, *Studies* 1:147-152. We might also note
     that William of St Thierry distinguishes two levels of unity of
     spirit: (i) willing what God wills, and (ii) being unable to will
     other than what God wills (see, for example, *Epistola ad fratres
     de Monte-Dei* II, iii, 15; PL 184:348A-349B [SCh 223:348-354; CF
     12:94-96]). Cp. also Henry of Clairvaux, *De peregrinante civitate
     Dei* iii; PL 204:282C.
77. See Sharif, ed., *A History* 1:369. The two forms of *fanā*ʾ are here
     translated as 'apparent annihilation' *(fanā*ʾ *al-ẓāhir)* and 'real
     annihilation' *(fanā*ʾ *al-bāṭin)*.
78. See Smith, *Readings*, 35.
79. See the *Shorter Encyclopaedia of Islam* 533, s.v. *shaṭḥ* for a list
     of the most famous *shaṭaḥāt* and further bibliographical references.
80. For the full text in translation, see W. H. T. Gairdner, trans.,
     Al-Ghazālī's Mishkāt al-Anwār (London, 1924; rpt. Lahore, 1952)
     106-108, and R. C. Zaehner, *Hindu and Muslim Mysticism* (London,
     1960; rpt. New York, 1969) 164-165.
81. For the Persian text, see M. Ṣabrī, ed., *Al-Jawāhir al-Ghawālī*
     (Cairo, A. H. 1353/A.D. 1934) 123. According to Gairdner, the
     whole of the *Mishkāt* may be regarded as expressing ideas which
     a mystic 'believes in secret between himself and Allah and never
     mentions except to an inner circle of his students' *(Al-Ghazālī's
     Mishkāt al-Anwar*, 19). Cp. also Ghazālī's comment at the beginning
     of his *Ihyāʾ* ʿ*ulūm ad-Dīn:* 'The concern of this book is with prac-
     tical knowledge *(*ʿ*ilm al-mu*ʿ*āmala)* only, rather than with contem-
     plative knowledge *(*ʿ*ilm al-mukāshafa)* which one is not allowed to
     set down in books, though it is the real purpose of the seeker'
     (see J. S. Trimingham, *The Sufi Orders in Islam* [Oxford, 1973]
     151).
82. See Zaehner, *Hindu and Muslim Mysticism*, 162-171. The question
     of how and to what extent Ghazālī's ideas changed and developed
     is a difficult and complex question. There are many who would
     disagree with Zaehner, but a full discussion is outside the scope
     of this present paper.
83. See M. Smith, *Al-Ghazālī the Mystic* (London, 1944) 202, quoting
     the beginning of ibn Ṭufayl's *Ḥayy ibn Yaqẓān*.
84. *Ibid.* Ibn Ṭufayl is here quoting Ghazālī himself.
85. *Ibid.* 203.
86. *Ibid.* The Sufi masters, in fact, very frequently distinguished
     between 'exoteric knowledge' *(al-*ʿ*ilm al-ẓāhirī)* and 'esoteric
     knowledge' *(al-*ʿ*ilm al-bāṭinī)*. It was one of the ways of avoid-
     ing the charge of *bid*ʿ*a* ('innovation,' and hence 'heresy').

37. For a full discussion which says all that could possibly be said, see Augustine, *De Genesi ad litteram* XII *passim*; PL 34:453-486, and for a brief summary, *ibid.* XII, vi, 15-vii, 16; PL 34: 458-9.

38. Smith, *Al-Ghazālī the Mystic* 190 (= *Readings* 69). This is also Jāmī's opinion, see Sharif, ed., *A History*, 2:873. Precisely the same idea is expressed by the Mādhyamika Buddhist term, 'the emptiness of emptiness' (see E. Conze, *Buddhist Thought in India* [London, 1962] 242-249). Junayd's *fanāᵓ ᶜan al-fanāᵓ* (see Sarrāj, *Kitāb al-lumaᶜ* 388) does not express quite the same idea.

39. Nicholson, *Studies in Islāmic Mysticism* 203 (I have changed Nicholson's translation of *dhāt* from 'selfhood' to 'essence' in order to maintain a consistent terminology).

90. See A. J. Arberry, trans., *The Mawāqif and Mukhāṭabāt of Muhammad ibn ᶜAbdi'l-Jabbār al-Niffarī* (London, 1935) 93 *(Mawāqif* 55,20). *Mawqif* is hereafter abbreviated M.

91. See *ibid.* 85 (M 49, 2); 49 (M 14, 14); 58 (M 21, 9); and elsewhere. (See *ibid.* 259 s.v. *dhikr* 'recollection' for a list of texts). *Dhikr* is actually an important technical term in Islām with a considerable breadth of meaning (see, for example, Schimmel, *Mystical Dimensions*, 167-178), but I am here more concerned with what is termed *dhikr bi'l-qalb (dhikr* with the heart = 'remembering') than with *dhikr bi'l-lisān (dhikr* with the tongue = 'mentioning' = the ritualistic repetition of certain formal phrases).

92. See, for example, Arberry, *The Mawāqif and Mukhāṭabāt*, 37 (M 8, 92); 48-49 (M 14, 10); 49 (M 14, 14); 98 (M 57, 13); 104 (M 62, 2). Other references may be found among the texts listed in *ibid.* 257, s.v. *hijāb* 'veil.'

93. See *De contemplando Deo* ix, 21; PL 184:378D-379A (SCh 61 *bis*:114-116; CF 3:62).

94. See Conze, *Buddhist Thought*, 61-66.

95. See, for example, Smith, *Readings* 101 (ibn ᶜArabī), and Jurji, *Illumination*, 70 (Abū'l-Mawāhib al-Shādhilī).

96. See Smith, *Readings*, 83 (ᶜAṭṭār).

97. See Bernard, SC 85, 13; PL 183:1194B (SBOp 2:315-316): 'In hoc ultimo genere interdum exceditur et seceditur etiam a corporeis sensibus, ut sese non sentiat quae Verbum sentit.'

98. Cp. P. Mamo, 'Is Plotinian Mysticism Monistic?' in R. B. Harris, ed., *The Significance of Neo-Platonism* (Norfolk, Va, 1976) 205-206: 'we cannot say, as Zaehner does, that since the soul of the mystic has survived the encounter, the experience of absorption was an illusion, nor that the self survives by nature, nor that some existential otherness remains at the very moment of union. It is not the soul or the ordinary ego that **survives**. The ego, even the ego established in the *Nous*, is lost, since the idea of an ego remaining in the absence of all multiplicity and differentiation is unintelligible. What remains is the admittedly

strange notion of a mind whose formal and intelligible structure is still intact (and still known by all other form-minds)
but whose normal self-awareness is lacking because it is now
"a mind senseless and in love".'

99. Space precludes a discussion of this interesting question at
the present time. A comprehensive examination of the idea
would have to include a discussion of the *turīya* state in Hinduism
and the very difficult question of *nirodha-samāpatti* in Buddhism.

100. G. Scholem, *On the Kabbalah and Its Symbolism*, trans. R. Manheim,
(New York, 1969) 8.

101. P. Merlan, *Monopsychism Mysticism Metaconsciousness* (The Hague,
1969²) 81.

102. *Ibid.* 80.

103. *Ibid.* 81-82. Much could be said on this matter, but this is not
a study of Plotinus. For a brief, useful, and stimulating investigation, see the article by Plato Mamo cited in n. 98 above.
Further bibliographical references will be found therein.

104. For a brief but sound consideration of the so-called 'formless
attainments' *(ārūpya-samāpatti)*, see H. V. Guenther, *Philosophy
and Psychology in the Abhidharma* (Delhi, 1974²) 126-134.

105. See Richard's *Benjamin Major* I, vi; PL 196:70B (and much of his
book IV; PL 196:135 foll.).

106. This is the goal of the Sāmkhya-Yoga system. For a discussion,
see R. C. Zaehner, *Hinduism* (London, 1966²) 67-72, 89.

MEDIEVAL FEMININE MONASTICISM:
REALITY VERSUS ROMANTIC IMAGES

Jean Leclercq

Historical Evidence and the Imagination

In a previous discussion of the genetic typology of feminine
monasticism in the Middle Ages, I first attempted to show how the
various monastic life-styles emerged from the cultural context in
which the different monasteries arose and evolved.[1] I tried to discern on the basis of these facts the main features and characteristics, the permanent elements and problems which existed throughout
the period. The two parts of this study are now being prepared for
publication.

Here I would like to show that this medieval period had, and
continues to have, an impact on the ideas--more precisely the images
--of what feminine monastic life is or should be in logical consequence of what it was in the middle ages. Now, many of our images
of medieval monasticism are marked by **two** characteristics. In the
first **place, they are only partially representative of real facts.**
Consequently, we must do our best to acquire a complete picture of
the full reality. In the second place, reality itself has been simplified, idealized, hardened, unified and thus become the object of
more or less stylized, uniform legislations. This process began in
post-medieval times, with the Council of Trent, and culminated in the
nineteenth century, so strongly influenced by romanticism.[2] There
are still some today who quite naturally project these simplified
images, not only on the medieval period itself, but also on our own
times in this last third of the twentieth century.

We are faced then with the necessity of disentangling these cultural elements, and of separating, not only historical facts, but also the later creations of the imagination, from the facts of the Gospel and true tradition. Such a necessity implies that we distinguish
between Gospel and culture and liberate present-day monastic life from
the shackles of the past, be it **authentic** or imaginary. To do so is
one of the urgent tasks facing us today. We must go about it in various fields: monasticism in general;[3] the exercising of authority and
the practice of obedience;[4] and in particular in the whole **complex** of
feminine monasticism.

Many of the images inherited from the nineteenth and the first
half of the twentieth century come from general histories. These have
their merits and until **recently** were the only ones possible. Fortunately today, monastic historiography is making progress, mainly by the increasing use of sociology, psychology, statistics, and even the use of
eletronic computers. Because of these new methods and means, and also

by reason of a more attentive consideration of the sources themselves,
instead of historical surveys or syntheses, it is now possible to
study, not only the history of institutions and the literary and doctrinal heritage of monasticism, but to see life as it really was, and
have a truer picture of real people, the monks who really existed.

To give an illustration straightaway and very concretely of the
way in which **people** tend to project so-called traditional--but in fact
modern--practices on ancient texts, including the Rule of St Benedict,
I would like to tell of a fact which happened in 1605, when Mother
Magdalen Morteska restored at Chelmo benedictine life for women in
Poland after it had disappeared during the Reformation.[5] The Consti-
tutions were the work of a commission composed of Bishop Peter Kostlea,
acting as the Holy See's sub-Delegate, Magdalen Morteska and four
other Chelmo Nuns, and some theologians and lawyers, most of them Je-
suits. When they came to the chapter in the Rule of St Benedict about
the habit, they read: *scapulare propter opera,* and they translated it,
'an apron for work,' so that the first generation of Chelmno nuns never thought they would permanently wear a scapular; they wore tunics
with belts, cowls in the choir, and aprons whenever necessary.

Later, however, the Carmelites' idea of a holy scapular, the most
important and sacred part of the habit, prevailed. It was almost a
reliquary. Besides, benedictine monks were indignant at the Jesuit interpretation of that text, which they judged incompetent. An abbot wrote
a long defence of the scapular, going so far as to state that it was
a point disputed among 'the theologians of our Order' whether it was
a mortal or a venial sin for a monk to go to sleep without a scapular!
In the end, most of the nuns' monasteries accepted the scapular and
sometimes this acceptance was celebrated very **solemnly.** St Benedict's
apron had become a benedictine ornament. I cannot help thinking, in
connection with this event, of a humorous remark made by a nun who
said that in the times of St Benedict, the scapular--*scapulare propter
opera*--was already no more than an 'opera dress'.

I would now like to mention some other items, more important than
the one I have just mentioned and deserving of being studied more thor-
oughly. Concerning several matters in history, we may apply, with
due modification, the words spoken by the Lord about the Truth which
he was and which he taught: 'History will make you free.' Free, that
is, from the past, from the 'traditions' which are often either recent
or pseudo-traditions. Today, the providence of God seems to be leading us to situations which are closer to real tradition rather than to
our imagination.

Size of Communities

The first point which comes to mind, because it is one of the
most obvious, is that of the size of the communities. Since the nineteenth century, many of us have imagined that the normal community

should be a large one and most monastic buildings have been designed
for about fifty members, at least. If we examine the facts in the
light of the statistics we are more able to establish, however, we
cannot help noticing that communities in the middle ages were generally much smaller than this. A few monasteries which, during **certain**
periods, had many members, have been taken as a normal example of
things in the majority of houses. Such exceptional cases were generally well-known through chronicles and other major documents.[6] But
if we examine cartularies and the detailed studies to which they have
recently given rise, we see that the general, normal state of affairs
was quite different. For example, in the cistercian nunnery of Rifred-
do in Northern Italy, between 1231-1334, the 'number of nuns was usually about twenty.'[7] In England, during the thirteenth and fourteenth
centuries, the average population of cistercian nunneries was some
10.03 and 12.4. It is remarkable that between 1168-1308, there were
one hundred twenty-three rebellions among the *conversi*. This makes
an average of one rebellion every fourteen months. In only five of
these revolts were *conversi*-nuns involved.[8]

In France in 1760, the average population in all monastic communities, was 23.7.[9] During the twelfth and thirteenth centuries, in the
cluniac **priories** of the province of Lombardy, the average number was
five.[10] J. Dubois had established that, during the middle ages, the
average members of monastic rural priories numbered two.[11] He **reached**
a similar conclusion in another study, mainly concerning male monastic
houses, which on the whole produced more documents than female houses
and have been the object of more frequent studies.[12] But the same results, it may be conjectured, would be established for nunneries. Also
to be taken into account is the fact that so far it is the major **monas-**
tic orders which have been studied. Much work remains to be done on
smaller orders, such as Tiron, and small groups or foundations which
either died out after one or several generations or else merged with
other orders, or simply survived without attracting the attention of
historians.

To sum up, I would say that one of the conclusions which I, as
an old historian, draw, is that monastic communities on the whole have
only been prosperous in large numbers of members during exceptional
periods, and that on the whole they had to remain faithful without
being numerous, and that often enough they succeeded in doing so.

The Impact of Nobility

As an historian has observed for certain monasteries of the
twelfth and thirteenth centuries, 'Nuns appear to have been relative-
ly few in number (fewer than monks): this may be due to their origin,
for they generally belong to noble families.'[13] It may be difficult
in the United States--less so in **Canada**, especially in the province
of Québec--to realize what may have been the enduring importance of

nobility in feminine monastic life and the forms of segregation which
were its consequences. More examples could be added to those which
have already been given elsewhere.[14] For instance, it seems very likely that St Gertrude the Great, in the second half of the thirteenth
century, could not become abbess at Helfta because she was not of noble birth.[15] This did not, however, prevent her from having lofty
spiritual experiences and a great theological message. Thus the value
of what she wrote did not come from any secular influence she might
have had but from her intrinsic gifts as a common sister. As this
was almost unthinkable, however, she was made a posthumous abbess in
the sixteenth century, thanks to an easy confusion with her own abbess,
St Gertrude of Hackeborn, and in the romantic nineteenth century, she
was considered 'the great abbess' *(die grösse Aebtissin)*.

Titles like 'The Lord Abbot,' 'The Lady Abbess,' 'Dom' and 'Dame'
with the meaning they were given in England during the late Middle
Ages, were in those times indications of the secularization of spiritual roles.

Another very typical example can be observed in the complex ser-
series of buildings which constitute the present dominican convent of
the Angelicum in Rome.[16] There were, a convent for noble nuns, a convent for non-noble ones, and a convent for those who had been converted
from Judaism or from other forms of life; and there was a fourth one
still elsewhere, not far away, in Humility Street *(Via dell'Umilità)*
where the North American College now is, for yet another category of
nuns. In the convent for noble nuns, the first floor--which is tradi-
tionally called in roman palaces the 'noble floor'--was occupied by
the nuns themselves. On the upper floor their servants lived, each
one having a kitchenette and, possibly in order to keep an eye on
their mistresses' wishes, a peephole in the floor. We know too, that
in Latin America similar situations have existed until comparatively
recent times. It was Pope St Pius V who built the convents in what
was to become the Angelicum, during a time of fervor after the reform
of the Roman Church. In Latin America each of the Spanish ladies who
entered the monastery had as a servant an Indian girl to whom she gave
a name and who worked for her in a kitchenette. Such Sisters were
called 'Sisters of Obedience' as if the nuns were not bound to obey.

And of course, it behooved them to be as elegant as became their
social condition. At the Abbey of Stanionski in Poland, each nun had
a hair-dresser bust to ensure that her hairstyle was becoming to her
particular form of beauty. The abbess had the right to have a painted
bust! There remain still today two collections of such busts. It may
well be that other forms of the nobility complex have survived and are
still in use in certain countries where affluent societies rub against
poorer. To be quite honest, I wondered whether this was not the case
when I first noticed that North American men religious called upon
Mexican nuns to do the kitchen and laundry work that nearby American
nuns declined to undertake.

Monastic Vocation and Virginity

As has been shown elsewhere, it was only during the nineteenth century that the Consecration of Virgins came to be associated with the Solemn Profession of Benedictine Nuns. The history of this question of virginal consecration can easily be illustrated by a few select *Lives* of a few illustrious abbesses and nuns; from hagiographical interpretations, it is only too easy to draw hasty doctrinal conclusions.[17] But such information must be complimented by other sources.

One group of such sources--which also forms a particular literary genre--is composed of the romances and poems telling us that wives of knights entered the monastery, either during their husband's life-time or after his death through war, accident or other cause. The formula used in such circumstances is that these women 'received the veil'. Sometimes it is explicitly stated that they did so out of fidelity to their deceased husband.[18]

To what extent is it possible to gain some accurate notion of the proportion of nuns entering the monastery after having lived in the married state? Another group of documents which would provide information on the subject is that of the cartularies: on the basis of the information they give statistics should be drawn up. In one of the rare studies which has already been done along these lines, concerning the benedictine abbey of St George at Ronceray, the Trinity at Caen, and the priory Marcigny, for the period covering the eleventh and twelfth centuries, it has been possible to draw up lists of dozens of nuns, each with her title and usually her connection with other members of her family. Some of these nuns are said to be the daughter of so-and-so, others are styled wife (*uxor*) or widow (*vidua*) or again mother (*mater*). For each of these nuns, irrespective of her previous civil status, the term used by historians is 'consecration'. These women were 'consecrated', and being consecrated was equivalent to receiving or taking the veil. The examples mentioned all concern women of noble origin. At Ronceray, among the seventy-three nuns whose names and titles are known to us, twenty-two were widows or matrons: the widows were twice as numerous as the wives. Widows and matrons represent 30.13% of the nuns.[19] For Marcigny we know of seventeen married ladies and seventeen widows. Together they represented more than half of the total community; precisely 53.30% had been married. And this, let it be remembered, was in a foundation of the reformed abbey of Cluny where stress was laid on authentic vocation.[20]

The reasons married women separated from their husbands to enter the monastery varied. Sometimes, we have as our only source romances and secular love poems; this was at least one means of freeing a husband and opening the way for him to marry another woman. The practical interpretation of canon law allowed for such cases, and there exist several documents to give evidence.[21] As for widows, the monastery afforded a lady bereaved of her husband a protection and material security which

secular society did not afford.[22] Other widows, as has been said, took
the veil out of fidelity to the memory of their deceased husbands and
thus were spared the obligation of contracting a second marriage. Such
psychological and spiritual dispositions gave rise to a few beautiful
poems in which we read such lines as: 'Out of love for you, I shall
be clothed with a garment of penitence, and renounce all the facili·ties
of life.'[23]

Cases of taking the veil through fidelity to a deceased husband
account for the high number of nuns who had been married. Although an
anonymous monk in Mainz in the twelfth century compiled a *Pontifical*
containing a ritual for the consecration of virgins, there were but
few manuscripts of this text, and they were in limited use.[24]

Forced Vocations and Happiness

During certain periods, many nuns had been brought to the cloister
in tender childhood. This does not mean that they never freely consent-
ed to their religious state and that they had no real vocation. But
there do seem to be cases where some such women never reached free acceptance, at least if we are to judge by poems such as the 'Complaint
of the Unhappy Nun'.[25] It is difficult to determine the extent to which
this facile satirical genre expressed a real situation or to which it
was merely the occasion for goliardic students to give vent to their
talent and entertain a secular audience. The most famous of these songs
beginning with the words, *Plangit nonna fletibus,* is preserved in a single copy in the Vatican Library.[26] It enters into concrete details whic
though amusing, render translation delicate. A more or less summarized
English version has been given in four stanzas of which the first two
read as follows:

> Poor me, poor nun
> shut out of the sun,
> deprived of all fun
> when life's barely begun!
>
> I crawl from my cell
> to swing that cracked bell,
> to gnaw a psalm stale,
> a bad canticle....

We are obliged to remark that such complaints of unhappy nuns are
few in number, fewer than those of women who were unhappy because 'badly married'. This would seem to confirm a fact observed by various historians:[27] the educational system and the social milieu seemed to have
favored the development of not only good monks, but also happy monks.
We have a very explicit witness for nuns dating from the seventeenth
century. It concerns Mère Angélique who, at Port Royal, became not only

a fervent nun, an abbess, but also a strict reformatrice. Her recent biographers write:

> She had been made a nun against her wish, which is clearly
> shown by a conversation she had had years earlier, when she
> said to her grandfather, M. Marion, that she was unlucky to
> be the second daughter, for if she had been the eldest, she
> would have been the one to be married. But having been made
> a nun against her wish, and by the very parents who now tried
> to oppose her resolution, she wanted to live the monastic
> life sincerely and make her sisters follow its rules in all
> their details with **unconditional** self-surrender.[28]

The Paradoxes of Enclosure

I have already dealt on other occasions with the problem of the
various forms, degrees of, and motivation for the enclosure of nuns.[29]
But it is worthwhile illustrating the topic with some other examples,
because it remains so easy to project on the past images formed in recent times.

For instance, cistercian nuns--contrary to what is sometimes as-
sumed--did not originally have grilles. This fact is authenticated in
the case of the nunnery of Coiroux founded by St Stephen of Obazine in
the twelfth century. These nuns only became Cistercians later by affili-
ation and were not typical of twelfth-century **cistercian** nuns, who seem
on the contrary to have had the same measure of enclosure as the monks,
under the authority of their abbess. Still in the thirteenth century,
the cistercian nuns of **Flanders** were not strictly enclosed: they went
to work in the fields; during the harvest time, they stayed several days
at the farms and granges; they went to town on business. None of this
prevented their communities from being among the most fervent in the
Order and producing the **famous** saints and mystics we know.

Since the eleventh century male superiors had been charged with en-
forcing the laws of enclosure. But this has not generally been the case in
the following centuries. From the second half of the fourteenth century
in Spain, we have the interesting case of an entire congregation of benedictine monks on which the law was imposed as it was on nuns--the Poor
Clares in particular--under pressure from the founder of the Abbey of
Valladolid, King Juan I.[30] He took special joy in seeing monks enclosed
in exactly the same way as **nuns**, with grilles, turns, and only one door
by which to enter and go out. The nuns were called *las beatas*, and the
monks *los beatos*. All this resulted from a reaction against the relax-
ation of the times which had not been at all remedied by the Bull *Bene-
dictina*, promulgated by Benedict XII. In order to avoid the danger of
monks going out excessively, either for business or to earn their living,
they were obliged to take 'a vow of being shut in: *el voto de encierra-
mento*'. Certain words not found in the Rule of St Benedict were intro-

duced into the formula of their profession: *stabilitas perpetuae inclusionis*. This formula was maintained until the suppression of the Congregation in 1835, even though in practice the law had fallen out of use. But, for a number of years, these monks were in charge of reforming monastic houses for women, and it was fairly evident that they imposed their own enclosure.

Of course, they had to ask for a dispensation, as a privilege, from their solemn vow of enclosure. Originally the only cases in which they were allowed to go out was in the event of 'epidemics, famine or fire'. But inevitably the door opened more and more to let them attend political or ecclesiastical meetings. Even the abbots were not allowed out during Advent and Lent. If monks did go out, they had to come back the same day and those who infringed the law of strict enclosure were put on bread and water for as many days as they had been absent. Only the physician and the *sagrador*, the man charged with bleeding the monks, were allowed to enter. Yet, a monk could stay with his mother or his sister in one of the church chapels, and he did not have to see them from behind grilles.

All this was initiated by a king and dispensation had to come from the pope. Today, when much thought is being given to granting nuns the same enclosure as monks, we have from the past at least one example of nun's enclosure being imposed on monks. Obviously, this point of view and its practical application depends on social and cultural circumstances alone. After the Council of Trent, under the influence of St Charles Borromeo, uniform enclosure for all nuns led to placing all female orders on the same level, despite varying traditions and needs. From this time onward, enclosure was considered to be of supreme value.

As for grilles, they are still to be seen in the streets of all the former Hispanidad, from northern California to southern Latin America: they are a heritage of the Hispano-Arabic cultures. Still today, as in the course of the Moslem occupation of Spain over several centuries, they are both an ornament and a reminder of the way the Moslems used to keep women at home. Outside these countries, the imposition of grilles on all cloistered nuns was not always easy. For instance, the story is told in Switzerland that when, during the eighteenth century a *nunzio* was sent to enforce the use of grilles, all the cantons immediately issued a decree forbidding ironworkers to make them. This is but one of many examples showing how people dealt with legislation, without denying it. Another story is told of an abbess and some nuns travelling by carriage to make a foundation. The abbess knew she would pass in front of her family house; she obtained permission to stop over, but not to get out. The carriage stopped under the entrance porch and, with her nuns, she enjoyed a banquet carried out to the carriage.

Sacramental Dependancy?

From the origins of monasticism until the twelfth century, monks
and nuns often made their confession to other monks and to abbots.
to nuns and to abbesses. If the 1228 General Chapter of the Cistercian
Order, and then, in the early fourteenth century[31] Boniface VIII, for-
bade abbesses to hear confessions,[32] it is because they were hearing
them. What had happened between the first half of the twelfth century
and the thirteenth-fourteenth centuries was that monastic confession
had been assimilated to, and replaced by the sacrament of penance:
this was part of what Fr Ladislas Orsy called 'the evolving Church'.[33]
Before that late period, nuns could manage without priests for that
purpose. For the Eucharist, they needed a priest. But manuscripts
preserved in the Vatican Library and elsewhere show that monasteries
of monks and nuns, in the tenth to twelfth centuries, were able to
have 'eucharistic celebrations without priests'.[34] Once bread and
wine had been consecrated, communities of monks and nuns could not
only receive, but 'take' Holy Communion as the central part of a liturgical service consisting of introductory psalmody, confession, litan-
ies, a series of prayers preparing for communion, accompanying it and
relating to it the sacrifice of the Mass, explaining its effects and,
finally, thanksgiving. It has always been taught that one of the effects of the Eucharist was the remission of sins and the healing of
their consequences. Thus, such liturgical services without priests
were both eucharistic and penitential celebrations. This practice
changed later, when theology changed, and when priests were supposed
to be numerous enough to say mass and hear the confessions of all the
monks and nuns. We know that during all the Middle Ages, many monasteries of monks maintained diocesan priests as chaplains *capellani*
to give them the sacraments.[35] But before that period, the sacramental dependence of monks and nuns on priests was different.

Feminine Promotion

The Problem of Motivation

H. I. Marrou, in a study which, although considered old by now,
is still valuable, gives us vast and precise information, highlighted
as always by the nuances that color his work, on the reasons which
led so many women in the first christian centuries to undertake a life
of virginity.[36] These conscious and explicit motivations have often
been formulated by writers in the Church and they are viewed as effect-
ing a total and exclusive union with Christ. But love for him is seen
also in preference to another form of union: that of marriage in a
society influenced by a non-christian past, a milieu which was in fact
still partially so and in which marriage as a status made its effects
felt very strongly. Its influence appeared in the practical sphere,

as women were felt to be an inferior species, and in the immoral behavior of many men, who displayed a violence to the point of brutal
eroticism, which understandably made refusal of marriage a defence
measure, a freedom, and a kind of promotion. As a reaction to this
immorality, there grew up both within and outside the Church, teachings on purity--different brands of Encratism--that disseminated an
abusive scorn for any sexual activity whatever.

It is not insignificant that an increase in the number of female
vocations at the end of the eleventh century coincided with the development of a new kind of literature--courtly or popular--in which were
sung the praises of a certain type of love termed 'pure', which was
for some people a cover for forms of refined eroticism. We can then
more easily understand that there were certain Christians who preferred
another way. There was another side to the coin, too, for in some
places we find evidence of purely spiritual friendships between monks
and nuns and other religious men and women.[37]

The heresies later to come under the generic term 'catharism'
had some points in common with the ancient 'dualistic theories' that
Marrou thinks 'explain the world and man by the action and reaction
of two opposing principles, the Principle of good and that of evil.'[38]
If Catharism put forward a way of escape from evil towards a 'purity'
which certainly had nothing to do with the Church's ideals, monachism
allowed, within orthodox structures, for the realization of an aspira-
tion which proceeded out of similar depths and which expressed the
same cultural phenomenon. The whole cultural context of medieval monastic vocations is still waiting to be studied objectively, without
prejudice and without the danger of reductionism.

One fact which must never be overlooked in the discussion of feminine monasticism in all periods of the Middle Ages, is that of steady
recruitment from the nobility, probably more intense at certain periods.[3]
Up to now, historians have studied different milieux in the light of historical texts--chronicles and accounts--and of spiritual tests--hagio-
graphy, doctrinal treatises, letters and other similar evidence. These
researches have thrown into relief some of the explicit motivations of
women who became nuns, together with those of members of their retinues.
Other motivating forces are seen at work in juridical texts, in particular in the solutions accorded to problems raised by the statutes for
nuns in canon law or by cases of married couples separating by mutual
consent in order to enter monasteries. There are types and degrees of
parental ties to be taken into account, rights of ownership and the dependence arising from it, according to different districts and periods;
feudal rights; there are women who were unable to marry, or who found
themselves abandoned by their husbands, legally or otherwise, when
they went off to wars and crusades. For some women, then, entry into
a monastery was a social refuge as well as an opportunity for spiritual
progress.[40]

The Cluniacs in Lombardy

There is, however, a type of document that has hardly been studied at all from this point of view. It consists of lists, compila-
tions of contracts and acts of sale, purchase, gift, or foundation
in which abbesses and nuns played a part. A recent, very strongly
documented study draws attention to this. It is limited in scope because it concerns only the Cluniac houses in Lombardy, but it is, in
fact, because of that all the more precise and it has paved the way
for a new avenue of research which might be undertaken along the same
lines.[41] In this study we see more clearly than elsewhere that the
monastic life was for many women not only a refuge from a society that
had little esteem for their sex, but also at the same time a way of
liberation from the restrictions and limits imposed on them by this
society. It was a way that held out to them possibilities of action,
of commitment, of fulfilling a more intense role within this same
society. Nuns found themselves on an equal footing with men. Many
experiences reserved to husbands had been forgone by women in the
world; in the cloister their privileges were to be acquired once husbands and secular life had been left behind.

This was manifest in different ways in different areas. In the
social scene, nuns enjoyed an autonomy which allowed them to act in-
dependently of men, whether clerical or married. They still had to
have the consent of an abbot or a lay 'adviser' who was charged with
looking after and defending their interests, but this was common to
monks and nuns everywhere. They were, however, allowed to act in their
own right, in their own name; they could sign documents in their capacity as abbesses and as nuns. In principle at least, and it appears
that this was often the case, decisions were taken after consultation
with the communities, as the Rule of Saint Benedict stipulates. And
although at the time specific evidence of women's participation in
the work of administration was rare, there are many lists which preserve Chapter deliberations, models of how women could exercise the
greatest responsibility, a thing they could never have done had they
been living in the world.

Such a situation had, like any other, its inconvenient side. Like
sequences in technological areas, to use a present-day expression,
in the improvement of lands, new methods of tillage, the construction
of canals, and above all in the building and upkeep of mills. The
nuns of Cantu had some five mills and they constituted their chief
source of revenue.[42] Administration, rentals, barter, investment
were all undertaken by the abbesses in person, even if this meant
that from time to time they had to leave the enclosure. The priest
has a spiritual role only, the administration of the sacraments,[43]
although sometimes for certain business transacted in places distant
from the monastery the nuns had to use their chaplain, monk or cleric,
as procurator. Even so, it happened sometimes that a community could

do without using a priest in this way for a period of ten years.[44]
Monasteries of nuns exercised a right of 'suzerainty' over their own
property and goods as well as houses; they accepted Church tithes,[45]
which they often received by act of law.[46] They were given donations
from private churches and had the right to nominate clerics or monks
as titulars.[47] The right of proprietorship gave the nuns the power
of coercion--*honor et districtio*.[48] In addition to all this was the
spiritual power radiated out from them to all the faithful and sometimes to the great and powerful. We know of recluses who were the
advisers of princes and kings, even in matters pertaining to the affairs of government.[49] The price of such fruitfulness of life was
the renunciation of sexual experience and maternity, so that mother-
hood might flourish in another form for these 'spiritual daughters'
as it did by means of prayer for the nuns of Cernobbio.[50]

This autonomous activity allowed nuns 'to live and make incarnate the Gospel message in their particular world'[51] and in their
particular social context. This was not of course held out as a motive for vocations but it happened as the normal consequence and fruit
of such a vocation, part of the 'hundredfold' which was promised and
given as a bonus. This activity, inherent in the monastic vocation
of nuns as well as that of clerics and monks, was accepted as such
and there was no attempt to deny it. It was integrated into the life
of the whole community above all when the foundation was made by a
woman or at woman's instigation--or implemented by individual nuns
when they were put in charge of the business of the monastery.

Such a situation had, like any other, its convenient side. Like
clerics and monks, nuns found themselves involved in contemporary
struggles which had the danger of limiting their spiritual intentions
and ends; a measure of secularization was a constant danger too for
them, with its attendant necessity for defending themselves against
it or of preventing it. **Incompetent** administration might put their
living at risk. The number of vocations admitted had to be confined
to the measure of community revenues.[52] It did happen that when certain Benedictines were unable to keep up their monastery, there was
an appeal to replace them with Poor Clares, who received rich donations.[53]

If a definite autonomy was recognized among nuns, it was because
they were seen to be capable of exercising it. It was in fact this
double recognition, juridical independence and the opportunity of
making use of it, that became more and more prevalent at the end of
the Middle Ages and afterwards was replaced by the canonists and, in
institutions, by the growing power of the Orders of men. And so the
entry of women into monastic life did not bring with it any lessening
of the esteem shown for their normal competence, but in fact occasion
was found for them to exercise this competence, occasions unknown to
their counterparts in the secular world. This was true not only for
abbesses and prioresses, who generally came from noble classes anyway

and therefore had the power of nobility, but is demonstrated by a collegiality of all the nuns meeting in Council or Chapter.

Conclusion: The Enduring Reality: Sponsa Christus

The formula *sponsa Christi* is found frequently in patristic and medieval literature. Inspired by many passages from the Old and New Testaments, it was first of all and principally applied to the whole Church, then much later, to each of its members, men or women, often indeed in its feminine grammatical form so that it was more easily associated with the word *anima:* the **individual** christian soul considered as the spouse of Christ. This was especially the case in the person of the Virgin Mary. In our day this way of speaking is reserved more and more for Christians who have given themselves to God in a special way in the religious life, particularly in the feminine monastic life. Books and documents testify to this.[54] It is a legitimate but a restrictive evolution; we must not forget that every christian person of whatever sex, celibate or not, is a member of the Church and with her a 'spouse' of Christ.[55]

If the formula carries this **universal** significance it does so in the first place only because it takes significance from the one without whom no one would have any right at all to be a member of the Church, Jesus the **Lord**. We have to put it in these general terms so that we are on our guard against language that is too technical and that is in danger of monopolizing, so to speak, by reason of its vocabulary and monastic style, a title which has an infinitely rich significance.

As a matter of fact, the problem has been raised in a penetrating study which has not received the attention it merits. Its author is a benedictine monk who uses a combination of three disciplines --medicine, psychology, and theology. He is Damien Debuisson of the Abbey of Pierre-qui-Vire.[56]

From premises borrowed from the philosophy of symbolism and pauline typology, he draws this conclusion: 'Union in the Holy Spirit of the Father and his Word is the Archetypal Source of union between Christ and his Church, between man and woman.'[57] He asks, 'if what is specifically original in male/female relationship cannot be transposed analogically to the supreme relationship of the Father and Christ? ...Is it possible to find in the submission of Christ to the Father not only filial **overtones** but "feminine" ones also, and cannot this be said not only of the Incarnate Word--as man--to God but even in the trinitarian relationship of the Word with his Father?' In short, a 'relationship of espousal' between the word of Christ and the Father.[59] This dialogue of love, this kiss exchanged in the Spirit are the exchange of **spouse** and **betrothed**. The author here employs the metaphor of the **kiss** used by the ancient Fathers and after them more recent theologians

from Scheeben to H. Mulhen and one which Bernard of Clairvaux also
developed in the twelfth century with exceptional precision.[60]   A
metaphor which does not say everything but which evokes an unfathom-
able aspect of the mystery of the Trinity, it is an archetype of
everything human, for *Ishsa*, the Word is 'the eternal Spouse the
creating Wisdom,' and 'the Son of God is by turn the Betrothed of
his Father and the Spouse of his Mother'.[62]

This can only be an inadequate summary of a long and very complex study, but at least it shows that there exists an interest in
research seeking to extend a tradition without being false to it.
In line with this then, it seems justifiable to speak of both aspects
of the mystery, of the *Sponsa Christi* and also of *Sponsa Christus*.
This is the language of a reality that attempts to set feminine monastic life in the context not only of the Church and of Christ but
also in the life of the Holy Trinity.

Abbaye Saint-Maurice, Clervaux

NOTES

1. 'Medieval Feminine Monasticism' will appear with the Proceedings of the Benedictine Conference held at St John's Abbey, College-ville, in June 1980; 'Problems of Feminine Monasticism,' in the Proceedings of the Benedictine Conference held at St Benedict Center, Madison, Wisconsin, in October 1981. In the following footnotes, titles which are not preceded by the name of an author are those of publications where I have dealt at greater length which can only be mentioned here.

2. 'Le renouveau solesmien et le renouveau religieux du XIXe siècle,' in *Studia monastica* 9 (1976) 157-195.

3. 'Evangile et culture dans la tradition bénédictine,' in *Nouvelle revue théologique* 104 (1972) 171-182.

4. 'Evangile et culture dans l'histoire de l'autorité monastique,' in *La vie des communautés religieuses*

5. K. Gorski, 'Mère Madeleine Morteska (1555-1631) et les origines de la réforme bénédictine en Pologne,' in *Studia monastica* 19 (1977) 387-406. To Sr M. Borkowska OSB I am indebted—and grate-ful—for the scapular story. The pamphlet of Fr Stanislaus Szcygie, abbot of Staze Trocki in Lithuania, tells about the scapular and the absolute necessity of having one.

6. Such figures are given, for instance, in P. Schmitz, *Histoire de l'Ordre de St Benoît*, VII (Maredsous 1956) p. 52.

7. Catherine E. Boyd, *A Cistercian Nunnery in Medieval Italy. The Story of Riffredo in Saluzzo, 1220-1300* (Cambridge, Mass., 1943) p. 107.

8. J. A. Nichols, 'The Internal Organization of English Cistercian Nunneries,' in *Cîteaux* 30 (1979) 32.

9. On the real size of monastic communities during the middle ages and later, J. Dubois, 'Du nombre des moines dans les monastères,' in *Lettre de Ligugé*, n° 134 (1969) 24-36.

10. J. Leclercq, 'Pontida e la vita nei monasteri Cluniacensi di Lom-bardia,' in *Cluny in Lombardia* (Centro Storico Benedettino Italiano, 1979) 435-436.

11. J. Dubois, 'Communication' in *Bulletin de la Société nationale des Antiquaires de France* (1977) p. 162.

12. On the life and prayer in small monasteries in the middle ages, J. Dubois, 'La vie des moines dans les prieurés du moyen âge, in *Lettre de Ligugé*, n° 133 (1969) 10-32; and 'Les moines dans la société du moyen âge,' in *Revue d'histoire de l'Eglise de France* 60 (1974) 19-22 and 33-34; 'Saint Guinefort vénéré des Dombes. Comment un martyr inconnu fut substitué à un chien-martyr,' in *Journal des savants* (1980) p. 152: 'In the houses where only two or three, sometimes only one, monk lived there was no litur-gical pomp. In the twelfth and thirteenth centuries, the monks were still content to have a simplified celebration of the divine

office. The saying of the breviary was as yet unknown, for it
only became widespread in the fourteenth and fifteenth centuries
and could only be enforced with the spreading of the printing
press.'

13. J. Verdon, 'Les moniales dans la France de l'Ouest aux XIe et
    XIIe siècles. Etude d'histoire sociale,' in *Cahiers de civilisa-
    tion médiévale* 19 (1976) 264.
14. Art. 'Nobilità,' in *Dizionario degli Instituti Perfezione* VI
    (Rome, 1980) col. 311-318.
15. P. Doyere, 'Introduction' in *Gertrude d'Helfta. Oeuvres spirit-
    uelles II, Le Héraut,* L. 1-II, Sources chrétiennes, 139, pp. 15-16;
    art. 'Gertrude d'Helfta (Sainte),' in DSp 6 (Paris, 1967) col. 332
16. Here I am summarizing information supplied by the dominican friars
    of the Angelicum which I also visited. On the life of dominican
    nuns in that convent in the seventeenth and eighteenth centuries;
    see A. Eszer, OP, 'Prinzessinen Chigi als Nonnen in den Klöstern
    S. Girolamo in Campani zu Siena und SS. Domenico e Sisto in Rom,'
    in E. Gatz, *Romische Kurie. Kirchliche Finanzen. Vetikanisches
    Archiv. Studie zu Ehren von Hermann Hoberg* (Rome, 1979) 171-196.
17. For example, Blessed Robert of Arbrissel (†1116), founder of the
    Order of Fontevrault, for his nunneries 'preferred to have a widow
    as superior rather than an unexperienced girl.' The first prior-
    ess, Horsende of Champagne, was the widow of William of Montsoreau;
    Blessed Robert gave her as coadjutrix Petronilla of Craon, the
    widow of Baron de Chemille; she became abbess in 1115 and founded
    houses; after J. Daoust, art. "Fontevrault,' in *Dictionnaire d'his-
    toire et de géographie ecclésiastique,* t. 17 (Paris, 1971), col.
    963, depending on *Baudry de Dol, Vita B. Roberti de Arbrisello,*
    16-21; PL 162:1051-1054. Other women, either widows or separated
    from their husbands by common consent, entered Cistercian nunneries
    or at Fontevrault sometimes with their daughter, and became prioress
    or abbesses; R. Pernoud, *La femme du temps des cathédrales* (Paris,
    1980) 132-153.
18. Texts are quoted by P. Scheuten, *Das Mönchtum in der altfranzö-
    sischen Profandichtung (12-14. Jahrhundert)* Münster-Westf., 1919)
    28-29.
19. J. Verdon, 'Les moniales dans la France,' p. 247-251.
20. *Ibid.,* p. 254.
21. P. Menard, *Les lais de Marie de France* (Paris, 1979) 146-147 with
    bibliography.
22. In *Monks and Love in Twelfth-Century France* (Oxford, 1979) 1-26,
    I have mentioned texts on this subject. Another example: accord-
    ing to S. Gregory, 'The Twelfth-Century Psalter Commentary in French
    for Laurette d'Alsace,' in *The Bible in the Middle Ages* (Louvain,
    1979) 122-123, Laurette d'Alsace became a nun after having had four,
    perhaps five, husbands.
23. Text in P. Bec, *La lyrique française au moyen âge* II (Paris, 1978)
    35-36.

24. J. Verdon, 'Les moniales dans la France', p. 260, with biblio-
    graphy.
25. On this literary genre, P. Bec, *La lyric française*, I: 74-75;
    II: 20-22, 34, 55.
26. Edition and English translation of the text in P. Droncke,
    Medieval Latin and the Rise of European Love-Lyric (Oxford,
    1968) II: 357-360.
27. For instance D. Knowles, John F. Benton, and among the most re-
    cent ones, Rousset, 'La femme et la famille dans l'<<histoire ec-
    clésiastique>> d'Orderic Vital,' in *Zeitschrift für schweizerische
    Kirchengeschichte* 63 (1969) 62; N. L. Brooke, *Marriage in Christian
    History. An Inaugural Lecture* (Cambridge, 1978) p. 35.
28. W. Roch, 'La Mère Angélique' in *Women Saints. East and West,*
    (Hollywood, Calif., 1955) 232.
29. Art. 'Clausura,' in *Dizionario degli Instituti di Perfezione* II
    (Rome, 1975) col. 1166-1171; to be published in French in *Col-
    lectanea Cisterciensia,* 42 (1980).
30. C. de la Serna, 'El voto de clausura en la Congregación de Val-
    lodolid,' in *Los consejos evangelicos en la tradición monastica,
    Studia Silensia* I (Silos, 1975) 142-182.
31. J. M. Canivez, *Statutae Capitulorum Generalium Ordinis Cistercien-
    sis,* II (Louvain, 1934) p. 248, 17.
32. *Corpus Iuris Canonici,* 1. VI, t. III, c. 16.
33. L. Orsy, SJ, *The Evolving Church and the Sacrament of Penance*
    (Denville, N.J., 1978).
34. Here will be summarized an article entitled 'Eucharistic Cele-
    brations Without Priests in the Middle Ages' in *Worship,* 1981,
    pp. 160-168.
35. 'Pontida e la vita monasteri cluniacensi in Lombardia,' in
    Cluny in Lombardia (Centro Benedettino Italiano, 1979) 435-436
    (in French in *Studia monastica,* 22 [1980] 29-42).
36. H. I. Marrou, 'L'idéal de la virginité et la condition de la femme
    dans la civilisation antique,' in *La chasteté,* Coll. 'Problèmes
    de la religieuse d'aujourd'hui' (Paris, 1953) 39-49.
37. Examples and references are to be found in the art. 'Amicizia'
    of the *Dizionario degli Instituti di Perfezione* [D.I.P.], I (Rome,
    1974) col. 516-520. The present article is one of a series of
    studies which I hope to pursue on the subject of feminine monas-
    ticism in the Middle Ages and of the influence which this period
    has had up to our day.
38. Marrou, p. 47.
39. See note 14.
40. Examples and texts are quoted in *Monks and Love in Twelfth Century
    France* (Oxford, 1979) and *Monks and Marriage in the Twelfth Century,*
    forthcoming from Seabury Press.
41. G. Andenna, *Il monachesimo Cluniacense femminile nella 'Provincia
    Lombardia,'* in *Cluny in Lombardia. Atti del Convegno di Pontido.
    22-25 aprile 1977,* (Cesena, 1979) 331-380, with pp. 331-332, a

a bibliography on the problems evoked in the preceding paragraph.
42. Andenna, p. 371.
43. *Ibid.*, p. 360.
44. *Ibid.*, p. 359.
45. *Ibid.*, p. 374, 376.
46. *Ibid.*, p. 375.
47. *Ibid.*, p. 359.
48. *Ibid.*, p. 352, 374.
49. *Medieval Women Recluses*, forthcoming.
50. Andenna, p. 364.
51. *Ibid.*, p. 370.
52. *Ibid.*, p. 338, 379.
53. *Ibid.*, p. 377.
54. C. Marmion, *Sponsa Verbi. La vierge consacrée au Christ* (Mared-
     sous, 1923). The words *Sponsa Christi* are the title and the open-
     ing words of an Apostolic Constitution by Pius XII, 21 Nov. 1950.
55. Bibliography in P. Adnes, 'Mariage spirituel,' in *Dictionnaire de
     spiritualité*, 10 (1977) col. 388-402.
56. D. Debuisson, 'Théologie mariale et mystère du couple (Perspectives
     de travail),' in *Eglise et théologie* 6 (1975) 195-240. These forty
     five pages are only part of a still unpublished study.
57. *Ibid.*, p. 209.
58. *Ibid.*, p. 210.
59. *Ibid.*, p. 217.
60. In *Monks and Marriage in the Twelfth Century*, Ch. VI: 'St Bernard
     and the Metaphor of Love,' in press, I have given texts.
61. Debuisson, p. 233.
62. *Ibid.*, p. 236.

NUNNERIES FOUNDED BY MONKS AND CANONS
IN TWELFTH CENTURY ENGLAND

Sharon K. Elkins

The opportunities for women to lead a full-time religious life increased dramatically in twelfth-century England. The thirteen nunneries at the beginning of the century, primarily royal foundations, almost exclusively in the southeast, were multiplied ten-fold, to one hundred thirty-five houses. A rich variety of institutional arrangements proliferated, serving women from many **strata** of society, in all **areas** of the country.

This paper describes one portion of this expansion: the religious houses for women in whose foundations monks and canons played a role.[1] Amid the total increase the activity of monks and canons was not of major importance--the dozen nunneries they founded account for only ten percent of the new establishments, twelve of one hundred twenty-two new houses. Yet, as this paper will argue, their significance was greater than the numbers themselves would indicate.

The nunneries founded by monks and canons were established in a very limited chronological period. These male religious began founding convents for women after another august group of churchmen had virtually stopped. In the first half of the twelfth century in England, bishops established eight nunneries and gained control of one other; only Ramstede was founded by a bishop after the midpoint of the century.[2] While most of the bishops' nunneries were founded before 1135, all the monks' and canons' nunneries were founded after that date, and at least nine of their twelve convents were established between 1135 and 1160. Indeed only St Mary de Pré was definitely founded after 1160, and it was an unusual house in that it was for leprous women.[3] These middle years of the century were a transitional moment in female religious life. Numbers of women settled in informal hermetic dwellings, without strict enclosure or supervision. Partly through the efforts of monks and canons, these informal arrangements were transformed into officially established and supervised priories.

The activity of these monks and canons sheds light on that troublesome problem of modern scholarship, the *frauenfragen*; what the society did with its women. In the 1930s, Grundmann **argued** that the early thirteenth-century Franciscans and Cistercians were reluctant to undertake the supervision of female religious.[4] Many historians now **claim** that the Franciscans and Cistercians were part of a broad pattern, in which celibate men found any involvement with women a risk and in which over-worked Orders rejected the time-consuming direction of female religious.[5] Any counterpoint to this apparently widespread sentiment becomes important, and the monks and canons of twelfth-century England appear to be notable exceptions.

Questions immediately arise. Why did these men agree to aid women when so few of their contemporaries were willing to do so? Are there any common circumstances which might explain their behavior? Is it possible that many male religious did not find supervising women a time-consuming, celibacy-threatening task? From these perpectives the dozen convents founded by monks and canons have an importance beyond their number.

The convents of Sopwell and Markyate were both closely associated with Geoffrey, abbot of St Albans from 1119 to 1146. Among his ambitious projects--the construction of a new shrine, a lepers' hospital, and a guest house--was the foundation of Sopwell priory. According to the *Gesta Abbatum*, by 1140, when Abbot Geoffrey became involved with Sopwell, two holy women had already made 'the poorest dwelling out of the branches of trees' near the woods called Eywood, not far from a river which widened there. 'They had begun to lead a life with vigils and prayers, under wondrous abstinence; and they had felicitously continued their new religious life *(novellam religionem suam)* with irreproachable chastity, enervating their bodies with bread and water.' Learning that the women had remained in this commendable way of life for several years, Abbot Geoffrey, 'persuaded by divine prophecy judged it suitable *(opportunas)* to construct there little dwellings *(mansiunculas)* for the woman.'[6]

The account in the *Gesta Abbatum* relates the gradual transformation, over the course of a decade, of this simple dwelling into a formally established priory subject to St Albans. When the two women were joined by others, Geoffrey had them 'veiled in the custom of nuns' and placed under the Rule of St Benedict and the patronage of the Blessed Virgin Mary. Over the years, 'inspired by the grace of God', Abbot Geoffrey increased the spiritual and temporal goods of the cell; and finally, before 1148, the fame of the place having grown, he took the final step: 'guarding the reputation and well-being of the nuns, having made there a house *(mansionem)*, he declared them to be enclosed there, under lock and doorbolt and the seal of the Abbot.'[7] Thereafter a maximum of thirteen chaste virgins, and no one else, was to dwell there; no one was to be received without the abbot and convent's permission; and the nuns were provided with a cemetary for their own use.[8]

The steps in this transformation are clear. Two holy women, who may or may not have made a formal profession, settled in the woods by a stream in the late 1130s; they attracted the attention of Abbot Geoffrey around 1140. As more women joined the first two, Abbot Geoffrey increased their material and spiritual possessions and regularized their life so that by 1148 there existed a priory of enclosed, veiled nuns dependent on St Albans. The *Gesta Abbatum* mentioned no pressing need of the women for this attention; they had lived felicitiously *(feliciter)* for several years before Abbot Geoffrey became their patron. The only motive given for Geoffrey's involvement was that he was 'persuaded by divine prophecy' and 'inspired by the grace of God'.

Some years earlier, around 1123, a young woman named Christina had inherited a hermitage from Roger, a former monk of St Albans. Around 1124, after Christina had sent Abbot Geoffrey a warning which a vision of his own confirmed, Geoffrey began to visit her, 'heard her exhortations, received her warnings, consulted her concerning uncertainties,...and suffered her rebukes'.[9] The details of their relationship have been outlined elsewhere[10] and are not particularly germane to this paper. Here we merely note that Christina's attachment to Geoffrey was said to have been at least as great as his to her; she was said to have 'refined him with great affection' and to have 'loved him with a wonderful but pure love'.[11]

Over the next two decades, this friendship had tangible results. Abbot Geoffrey gave Christina and the other women with her at the hermitage of Markyate some rents and tithes which belonged to St Albans, an alienation which did not please all his monks, and he constructed and later repaired buildings for the women.[12] In 1131, Christina made her public profession of virginity at St Albans in the presence of Alexander, Bishop of Lincoln.[13] And partly through the efforts of Abbot Geoffrey, in 1145 Christina and her successors obtained from the canons of St Paul's, London, ownership of the site. With the dedication of its church later that year by Bishop Alexander, the monastery of the Holy Trinity was recognized as a priory. The canons of St Paul's retained certain rights. Although the nuns could elect their own head, called *magistra,* rather than prioress or abbess, the canons' assent was needed, and the *magistra* and all the nuns had to swear *fidelitatem et indempnitatem,* that they would be loyal to the canons and in no way curtail their rights. In recognition of the canons' role in the foundation of the monastery, the nuns were to pay them three shillings each year.[14] The process was strikingly similar to the development at Sopwell: women living in a hermitage eventually became professed nuns in a formally recognized benedictine monastery after male religious became interested in their welfare.

Both St Albans and St Paul's, London, aided other female foundations. In 1194 Abbot Warin of St Albans established St Mary de Pré for some leprous women; he had the women veiled and 'constricted them by certain limits of a rule, lest wandering around they become involved in secular errors'.[15] A canon of St Paul's, Robert fitz Gelran, assigned to the prebend of Holywell, gave a piece of land where the church of St John the Baptist was located, namely 'the moor on which the spring called Holywell rises,' to nuns living in that church.[16] St Paul's, London, must have approved the alienation of land, a small tract only three acres in size, since one of Robert's successors in the same prebend, a precentor of St Paul's,

doubled the grant.[17] Holywell remained poor, but by the mid 1160s,
twenty to thirty years after Robert's gift, some twenty women were
struggling to survive there.[18] Although the women were first mentioned in the charter recording Robert's gift, they were already
living at the church before they received legal ownership of the
land. Thus both St Mary de Pré and Holywell were founded to aid
particular women, and at Holywell the women were called nuns and
said to be serving God there at the church.

Common elements link the three houses of Sopwell, Markyate,
and Holywell, all established near London in the 1130s and 1140s,
with Kilburn, a fourth convent, situated a few miles from that
city. Shortly before 1140, Herbert, Abbot of Westminster, and Pri-
or Osbert of Clare, granted 'to the three girls, namely Emma, Gunil-
da, and Christina, the hermitage of Kilburn which Godwyn had built,
with all the land of that place'.[19] Godwyn agreed to the transfer,
and more: Abbot Herbert appointed him '*magister* of the place and
custos of the girls as long as he lives'.[20] Upon Godwyn's death,
with the counsel of the abbot, 'the convent of girls will choose a
suitable senior, who will preside over their church'.[21]

In addition to consultation on the choice of a master and chaplain, the monks of Westminster had other rights over Kilburn. The
abbey retained custody of the place 'lest its rights be harmed by
anything rash or its rule by anything perverse'.[22] Gilbert, Bishop
of London, confirmed that the 'cell of Kilburn' was 'under subjection
and jurisdiction' to Westminster and exempt from his jurisdiction.[23]
The form of endowment provided by Westminster made the dependence
visible; in addition to the site, the girls were given two *beneficia*,
later specified as bread, ale, wine, mead, and a pittance (the daily
allotment of vegetables).[24]

A familiar sequence is discernible at Kilburn: women, in this
case referred to as *puellae*, inherited a hermitage with the aid of
a nearby monastery. Since the hermit who had built the dwelling remained with the women as master and chaplain, there may have been a
personal friendship predating the establishment like that between
Christina of Markyate and the hermit Roger. Like Holywell, Kilburn
remained poor, virtually a dependent cell of Westminster; it never
reached the independent status of Markyate.

The most detailed account of this development was provided in
the foundation charter of Thetford by abbot Hugh of Bury, who wanted
future generations to know that women had been 'rationally and order-
ly' introduced. According to Abbot Hugh, the cell of St George at
Thetford had been held by Bury for many years, supposedly from the
days of Canute. Through the death of its canons one by one and the
dissipation of its goods, Thetford had become so diminished that it
seemed more a deserted house than a dwelling of religious men. Around
1160, the only two remaining canons, Folcard and Andrew, complained
to abbot Hugh of the intolerable poverty of the place where they no

longer could, or would, remain. When Hugh objected that the deser-
tion of a place where religious had lived for so long would cause a
scandal, the two canons pleaded that the cell be ceded to certain
women who were leading a religious life at Ling in Norfolk with only
a few possessions. By combining the sparse possessions of the women
with those of Thetford, the place could be relieved from poverty and
recalled to religious rule.[25]

Abbot Hugh described his reaction to this suggestion:

> We greatly desired the improvement of (Thetford), but
> nevertheless we drew off from receiving so suddenly in
> the place those women *(foeminae)*, for by this they were
> called; partly because they were women, whose sex was not
> customary in that place, but primarily because we had
> nothing certain concerning their life and customs.[26]

It was problematic enough to introduce women (who again are not called nuns), but it was unthinkable to deal with women of uncertain character. In the foundation charter Hugh recounted his investigation of
the women's religious reputation. William Turbis, Bishop of Norwich,
commended the life and *conversatio* of the women in the strongest terms,
'for he had known them as if they were his disciples'. They had received 'from his hand the habit of religious and from that reception
had lived religiously in his parish'. Jeoffrey, archdeacon of Canterbury and the keeper of the king's seal, interceded on their behalf.
And William of Camera, sheriff of Norfolk and Suffolk, testified to
their honesty, for 'he had known them both under the religious habit
and before they had received it', and he had even sustained them with
his alms.[27]

The foundation charter recounts the day of transfer. The canons
resigned everything from the cell--all the moveables and everything
in pasture, pannage, arable land, and rents--into the hand of abbot
Hugh. With 'the canons standing there still and not only not recant-
ing but pleading with good will that it be done,' Thetford 'was conceded to the often mentioned nuns, into the hands of their prioress
Cecilia'. Abbot Hugh added two parish churches which Bury held in
the villa of Thetford, its rights to a field, and everything else
which the monastery held within and without Thetford. In recognition of this grant, the nuns were to pay Bury four shillings a year.[28]

Following the now familiar pattern, Thetford was subject to the
founding monastery. Upon granting Thetford to Cecilia, abbot Hugh
accepted from her a faithful promise, offered 'without sorry or fraud,'
that 'no work counsel, either by her or any other person' would scheme
to deprive Bury of what was owed. Because Thetford had been 'a member' of Bury 'up to this day', and because its loss would be like
cutting a limb from the body, Cecilia swore 'faith and obedience' to
Bury 'as to a mother church', saving only the obedience owed to the

bishop of Norwich, 'as to a spiritual father'.[29]

A summary of events at Sopwell, Markyate, Holywell, Kilburn, a and Thetford reveals the following features. After women had undertaken a life of prayer, with only meager resources and sometimes without formal vows, they attracted the attention of certain male religious who convinced their monastery to provide additional endowments and sponsor the women in a dependent cell or priory. Sometimes the bishop or another religious house aided in the formal establishment of the priory. After setting up a convent with its own church, the founding monastery retained certain rights over the election of the female head, the admission of nuns, and in some cases the selection of a master or chaplain. Temporal ties often remained, at times even direct subsidies of food, and in several cases the founding monastery remained responsible for the spiritualities of the daughter house. While each of the five convents deviates slightly from this mold, the general pattern is discernible.

Less is known about the other six nunneries founded by monks and canons, but the preserved details fit the pattern. A brief sketch should suffice. The abbot of the augustinian canons of Darley was responsible for the nunnery of King's Mead. In a confirmation charter of around 1160, the bishop of Coventry conceded to the abbot of Darley 'the care of the virgins whose house *(habitaculum)* the same constructed' about a mile from Darley. The bishop continued, 'and we give to that abbot freedom to consecrate virgins whose care we commit to him'.[30]

St Michael, Stamford, was envisioned as a large convent of up to forty nuns by its founder William of Waterville, abbot of Peterborough. Around 1155, William founded and built for the nuns a church which he retained 'in our subjection and counsel, concerning the disposition of its things both internal and external'. A warden *(praelatus)* was to be chosen and removed at the discretion of the abbot and his chapter; the abbot and chapter's permission was necessary for the election of a prioress and the reception of nuns. In every way the nuns and all their goods were to be arranged by the disposition of the abbot of Peterborough, lest on account of the increase of Stamford, the abbey of Peterborough suffer any detriment. As a sign of their subjection, the nuns of Stamford paid Peterborough half a mark annually on the feast of St Michael.[31] Whatever motivated the abbots of Darley and Peterborough to found nunneries, they retained extensive responsibilities. While little is known about Grimsby in Lincolnshire, there is some hint that it too was subject to its founding monastery.[32]

The remaining three convents--Blithbury, Crabhouse, and Farewell --contained women allied with hermits before the establishment of an official priory. Two monks named Saxe and Guthmund associated some nuns with them at their hermitage. As the records soon begin to refer to Blithbury as a house for nuns, it is likely that the men

transferred possession of the place to the women, as happened at
Markyate and Kilburn.[33] Crabhouse had a complicated history center-
ed around a few hermitesses who repeatedly found and lost patrons
in the middle years of the century; finally, sometime before 1180,
Roger, prior of Ranham, granted one of the surviving women, Lena,
a hermitage which eventually became subject to the cluniac house of
Castle Acre.[34] Farewell became a female house when brothers there
--Roger, Geoffrey, and Robert--transferred their possessions to
certain nuns and women devoted to God about 1140; the canons of
Lichfield were involved in the transactions.

Why did these men agree to aid women when so few of their contemporaries were willing to do so? Personal acquaintance seems to
be a crucial factor. These nunneries were not founded by monastic
orders, deciding in principle on the wisdom of admitting women to
their congregations. Rather, some independent benedictine monasteries, a cluniac priory, and a few augustinian canonries agreed to
provide for a few particular women known to members of their congregation, often to the abbot **himself**. Male hermits often played a
central role both in providing a site for women and in bringing them
to the attention of the monastery. Individual men **responded** to individual women who, for the most part, had already undertaken a devout life, had already proven their worthiness, before the monastery became involved.

The chronological period in which these foundations took place
is limited almost exclusively to the middle years of the century,
between 1135 and 1160. Several reasons for this suggest themselves.
At the start of the period, only a few nunneries existed in England.
By 1135, the thirteen convents for women in 1100 had more than **doubled**
to twenty-**nine**, but this was still a small number for the whole country. With so **few** alternatives available, monks and canons may have
felt the **responsibility** for providing material and spiritual services
for women who could not simply be sent elsewhere. Moreover, women
interested in a full-time religious life often had to set up house-
keeping on their own, perhaps by persuading a friendly hermit to
give them a dwelling and spiritual advice, and thus creating the
personal bonds and proving the virtue necessary to attract the spon-
sorship of male religious. By 1154, there were eighty nunneries in
England. After the first flush of enthusiasm for the monastic life
paled in Western Europe, the need to provide women with still additional convents may have **diminished**.

Was the task of aiding women time-consuming and burdensome? The
examples suggest that it was. In addition to alienating property
from their own monastery, the men assumed continuing responsibilities for the daughter foundation: the abbot frequently oversaw the
election of the prioress and the reception of nuns; a *custos* or master might be taken from the congregation of the parent monastery.
Sometimes the daughter house, poorly endowed, remained visibly

dependent on weekly allotments of food from the men's monastery.
Over the course of time, what had begun as a service to particular women undoubtedly became formalized into an institutional tie
which could become irksome when finances were strained, men and time
in short supply, and other religious vocally unwilling to be bother-
ed with the supervision of women. Some might suggest that the men
themselves, however inadvertently, created the situation which became onerous. Initially women of meager resources adopted lives of
prayer in an informal setting; the monks and canons formalized the
structure and insisted on subjection to a parent house. Had the parent monastery founded a strong, well-endowed, independent convent,
or left the women along, a burdensome dependence would never have
developed. But the need to provide women with priests, and the common assumption of the period that women required supervision and
care meant that a female house could become a drain on its parent.
In such circumstances, it is not surprising that, as the century progressed and the institutional demands became better known, fewer
male religious accepted the burden.
Even though the nunneries founded by monks and canons formed
only a small percentage of the new female foundations in twelfth-
century England, they may point to a wider trend. In these well-
documented monastic foundations, we catch glimpses of women taking
up a religious life on their own, even when they lacked financial
resources or ecclesiastical supervision. Women and men were found
cooperating in informal hermitages outside the structured monastic
establishments. Perhaps similar activities underlay some of the
less well-documented foundations for women by lay people. The accounts preserved by monasteries may give us one of our only furtive
glances at what could have been a larger movement of women on their
own initiative deciding to live a life of poverty and prayer.

Wellesley College

NOTES

1. See the list of foundations in David Knowles and Neville Had-
   cock, *Medieval Religious Houses, England and Wales*, 2nd ed.,
   London, 1971 and my dissertation, 'Female Religious in Twelfth
   Century England,' Harvard University, 1976. The twelve convents discussed in this paper are St Mary de Pré, Sopwell, Markyate, Holywell, Kilburn, Thetford, King's Mead, Stamford, Grimsby, Blithbury, Farewell, and Crabhouse. Although the three
   houses for Premonstratensian canonessess--Broadholme, Guyzance,
   and Orford--may have been established by Premonstratensian canons, the evidence is too scanty to include them.
2. St Sepulchre, Canterbury; St Margaret's, Ivinghoe; Stratford at
   Bow; St Radegund, Cambridge; Brewood; Farewell; Haverholme; and
   St Clement's, York were apparently founded by bishops, although
   the evidence is in some cases ambiguous. Chatteris was transferred to the jurisdiction of the bishop of Ely. Elkins, 'Female Religious,' 45-50, 110-113, 167.
3. *The Victoria History of the County of Hertford*, ed. William
   Page, vol. 4 (London, 1914) 428-9. Henry Thomas Riley, ed.,
   Gesta Abbatum Monasterii Sancti Albani, vol. 1 (London, 1867)
   199-204.
4. Herbert Grundmann, *Religiöse Bewegungen in Mittelalter* (1935,
   rpt. Hildesheim, 1961) especially chapters four and five.
5. See Catherine Boyd, *A Cistercian Nunnery in Mediaeval Italy*,
   (Cambridge, Mass., 1943) 72 ff; R. W. Southern, *Western Society and the Church in the Middle Ages* (Harmondsworth, 1970)
   312-318; Hane Tibbetts Schulenburg, 'Sexism and the celestial
   gynaeceum from 500 to 1200,' *Journal of Medieval History* (1978)
   117-133; and Brenda M. Bolton, *'Mulieres Sanctae'*, in Susan Mosher
   Stuard, ed., *Women in Medieval Society* (Philsdelphia, 1976) 141-
   158. Even popular histories have developed this theme, as in
   Frances and Joseph Gies, *Women in the Middle Ages* (New York,
   1978) 87-96.
6. *Gesta Abbatum*, 80-82; the account in *VCH, Hertfordshire*, 4:422-
   423 introduced unnecessary confusion between Sopwell and Markyate
   priories.
7. *Gesta Abbatum*, 81.
8. *Gesta Abbatum*, 81-82.
9. C. H. Talbot, ed., *The Life of Christina of Markyate* (Oxford, 1959)
   138. See also pages 134-193.
10. Christopher J. Holdsworth, 'Christina of Markyate,' in Derek
    Baker, ed., *Medieval Women*, (Oxford, 1978) 185-204; Talbot, pp.
    28-31.
11. Talbot, p. 138. Christina is said to have called Geoffrey *pre-
    cordialem suum, religionis amicus, carissimum, familiarissimum*
    and especially *dilectum*. See Talbot, 140-50.

12. *Gesta Abbatum*, 103.
13. Talbot, pp. 15 and 146-7.
14. William Dugdale, *Monasticon anglicanum*, edd. John Caley, Henry Ellis, and Bulkeley Bandinel, vol. III: London, 1846, 372.
15. *Gesta Abbatum*, 203. See note 3 above.
16. Dugdale, 4:393; *VCH Middlesex*, 1 (1969) 174-175.
17. *Ibid.*
18. Adrian Morey and C. N. L. Brooke, ed., *The Letters and Charters of Gilbert Foliot* (Cambridge, 1967) 245. In this letter to Robert de Chesney, bishop of Lincoln, Gilbert pleads that the women be allowed to retain the church of Dunton since they were dependent on it for their livelihood.
19. Dugdale, 3:426. A later tradition identified the girls as maids of honor to Matilda, wife of Henry I. See also Dugdale, 3:422, *VCH Middlesex*, 1:178-179, and *MRH* p. 259.
20. Dugdale, 3:426.
21. *Ibid.* The *custos* did not have to be from Westminster priory.
22. *Ibid.*
23. Morey and Brooke, *Gilbert Foliot*, 491.
24. Dugdale 3:426-7.
25. Dugdale, 4:475, 477-78; *MRH*, pp. 266-267. Since William Turbis was 'of blessed memory' by the time the charter was penned, it had to have been written more than a decade after the events it described.
26. Dugdale, 4:477-8.
27. *Ibid.*
28. *Ibid.*
29. *Ibid.*
30. Dugdale, 4:302, citing a previous edition. At least by the late twelfth century, the nuns of King's Mead had a *magister*. See Isaac Herbert Jeayes, *Descriptive Catalogue of Derbyshire Charters*, (London, 1906) p. 302; *VCH Derby*, 2 (1907) p. 43; *MRH*, p. 258
31. Dugdale, 4:260. A charter preserves a covenant by a prioress of Stamford in which she renews the subjection of the nunnery to Peterborough; Dugdale, 4:261. See also *VCH Northampton*, 2 (1906) 9
32. *MRH* p. 280 for the relationship between Grimsby and the Austin canons of Wellow.
33. Dugdale, 4:160; *VCH Stafford*, 3 (1970) p. 220. In this instance, the donor who granted the original site to the two men is also known.
34. For the involved tale, see *VCH Norfolk*, 2 (1906) p. 408 and Mary Bateson, 'The Register of Crabhouse Nunnery,' *Norfolk Archaeology*, 11 (1892) 1-71, especially pp. 2-7.
35. *VCH Stafford*, 3:222-3; Dugdale, 4:111. Since Bishop Roger de Clinton endowed the site and approved the transfer, he should be considered the founder of the monastery, as I indicated in footnote two. But the activity of the male religious also warrants treating this house on a par with Blithbury.

ARISTOCRATIC FAMILIES: FOUNDERS AND REFORMERS OF MONASTERIES IN THE TOURAINE, 930-1030

Mary Skinner

Count Gerald of Aurillac outfitted a beautiful monastery in the late ninth century and died in the faith that monks would be forthcoming to fill it.[1] The benedictine reforms intiated by St Odo of Cluny, our source for Gerald's expectations, did much to provide monks there and in the Touraine in the early tenth century. Counts like St Gerald, and lesser lords with the means to do so, desired to match their castles with monasteries providing liturgies for the living, prayers for the dead, and alms for the poor. I would like to examine the involvement of lay members of aristocratic families in the Touraine in the founding or reform of ten monasteries between 930 and 1030. Secular canons from these same families usually supported these benedictine reforms and their participation will be analyzed in a subsequent paper.

Only three monastic houses, Cormery, Villeloin and St Loup, apparently survived the. Viking invasions, and St Loup, the only monastic house for women in the Touraine, seems to have been defunct by 950.[2] Cormery and Villeloin were under the influence of the count of Anjou, whose brother was at one time abbot of both.[3] After a Viking massacre in the ninth century, monks from Marmoutier had been replaced there by secular canons from the Abbey of St Martin.[4]

The carolingian aristocrats who survived the Viking invasions and even increased their allodial lands in the late ninth century can be recognized by characteristic first names. The higher echelon provided counts, viscounts, and archbishops who were peers of the Robertian dukes, who became the Capetian kings. Some lesser families became independent lords with their own castles; one of the most notable, the Corbo-Arduins held the archbishopric for a time. Others were castellans, vassals, and knights by the late tenth century.[5]

The movement to found benedictine monasteries in the tenth and early eleventh centuries in the Touraine had four phases. In the tradition of St Martin, monks in the Touraine until the carolingian reforms of Benedict of Aniane lived in small semi-eremitical communities. The benedictine foundations of Cormery and Villeloin were under the auspices of the king.[6]

The first phase of the tenth century reforms followed the Viking invasions by thirty years. Its sponsors, Archbishop Teotolo and his sister, with the inspiration of Abbot Odo of Cluny, poured all their family lands into reestablishing the ancient Abbey of St Julien under the benedictine Rule.[7]

In the second phase, St Florent (958), Marmoutier (987) and Bourgueil (990) were all established by Counts Tetbald and Odo and their families. Count Odo in the late tenth century seems to have favored the benedictine Rule as a means of centralizing his author- ity. His relative, Gauzbert, in the 990s was abbot of St Julien, Bourgueil, Marmoutier, and Maillezais in Poitou. In the foundation charter of Bourgueil, attributed to Gauzbert, counts were said to follow in the footsteps of the apostles in their responsibility for the church.[8]

The third phase of the reforms was initiated by Herveus, treas- urer of St Martin, who may have been a relative of the powerful lords of Amboise and Buzançais. In the early eleventh century he founded Beaumont, to restore religious life for women in the Touraine, and St Côme, which drew monks from Marmoutier and may have been a retreat for canons of St Martin who wished to live a stricter life.[9]

In the final wave of foundations in the early eleventh century, local lay aristocrats made new benedictine **foundations** on their fam- ily lands in the countryside at Noyers, Tavant, and Preuilly. In- cluded in this group would be Beaulieu, founded by Fulk of Anjou shortly before his son, Count Geoffrey Martel, captured the Touraine in 1044.[10]

The reforms, then, were initiated successively by archbishop, count, treasurer of St Martin, and finally by lesser lords in the countryside. They were supported by donations by their followers and *fideles*. The pattern of monastic foundations reflects the dis- tribution of power in the Touraine. As authority and wealth became more decentralized, the level of society at which monastic founda- tions were made diminished.

Episcopal Initiative: The Abbey of St Julien

In the charters it is possible to discern the group of people behind the restoration of the ancient Abbey of St Julien, and even to sense the enthusiasm they had for the venture. Archbishop Teo- tolo, who made the foundation, was a close friend of Abbot Odo of Cluny; they may have been youthful canons of St Martin together.[11] Teotolo may even have been a monk of Cluny before becoming archbish- op. Teotolo and his sister Gersindis, perhaps the last of their line in a prominent carolingian family, gave the new foundation ex- tensive lands inherited from four uncles. Teotolo traded, bought, and sold these lands, especially many new vineyards, to make sure the new house would have an economically viable endowment. Most trading was made with canons of St Martin and their relatives, but certain lay people, perhaps of humble status, such as *Guimberones carpentarius*, also participated.[12]

St Odo and Teotolo were joined by prominent laymen of the Touraine, some of whom were converted to the monastic life. Erkem- bald renounced secular life to become one of the founding monks of St Julien. He was patriarch of a family who boasted among their

members Robert, an archbishop of Tours until 932, and who later became lords of Amboise and **Buzançais**. Erkembald's sons, Robert and
Girard, who became special bishop of St Martin continued to support
St Julien with donations of land. Abbot Gauzbert of St Julien, and
Herveus, treasurer of St Martin, key persons in the **benedictine** reform movement, may have been members of this family, one of the most
powerful in the Touraine.[13] Erkembald was not the only convert: Ful-
culfus, another prominent aristocrat of the Touraine, also renounced
his worldly possessions to become a monk of St Julien, making a substantial donation in the process.[14]

Lands traded, purchased, and donated, flowed in. In mid-century
a woman named Adalsindis and her two sons sold two small vineyards
to St Julien.[15] A decade later Bernardus, vassal and *fidelis* of Archbishop Arduin, gave the abbey a mill and its surrounding lands. He
may have been the same Bernardus who, with three laymen and a priest,
gave St Julien various vineyards.[16] Two *fideles* of Count Geoffrey
of Anjou, Gislardus and Gaufredus, added groves, meadowland, and an
aquaduct to the holdings of St Julien in 960 and 978.[17] Nephews of
Archbishop Arduin, Guandalbertus, Corbo, and another Arduin, contributed allodial vineyards, a manse, tithes and other revenues they
had been collecting unjustly on lands of St Julien.[18] Like Cluny,
St Julien was supposed to be free of lay interference under an abbot
elected by the monks. Unlike Cluny, it was to remain under the jurisdiction of the Archbishops of Tours, which soon led to some exploi-
tation on the part of Archbishop Arduin's nephews.[19]

In 990 Letaldus, a poor miller, gave the monks his mill, genero-
sity which after his death resulted in the destitution of his family.[20]
A few years later, a very prominent aristocrat, Gualterius, whose family had held the offices of viscount and vicar of Tours and treasurer
of St Martin, gave at small rent to St Julien vineyards that had been
given to him.[21] In 999 Corbo, now styling himself noble knight, gave
the abbey additional cultivated lands and vineyards.[22] Through the
tenth century St Julien won support from all groups in society, although lay relatives or *fideles* of Archbishops Teotolo and Arduin,
Counts Odo of Tours and Geoffrey of Anjou and the Erkembald-Robert
family made the most substantial donations. What the archbishops
had given, however, the archbishops could evidently take away, and
the relatives of Archbishop Arduin were for a while enriched with
lands and revenues of St Julien which they reluctantly returned to
the monks after their uncle's death late in the tenth century.[23] Such
restitution of monastic lands that had been alienated to the laity
or secular clergy became an integral part of the benedictine reform
movement in the late tenth and eleventh centuries.[24]

Although St Julien may have lost some of its first fervor in
the mid-tenth century, it was restored to discipline under Abbot
Gauzbert near its end; Gauzbert contributed to the benedictine reform at Marmoutier, and St Julien, like Cluny, spread the new

reforming spirit to neighboring houses.[25] St Odo of Cluny and St
Mayolus personally molded the life and spirituality of St Julien
and of Marmoutier.

St Odo's connections with Tours and St Julien are particularly
noteworthy. Likely the son of Ebbo of Deols in Berry,[26] a pious
lawyer, Odo was commended for military training to Counts William
of Aquitaine and Fulk of Anjou, and he may have lived for a time at
each of their courts. His father had also dedicated the infant Odo
to St Martin however, and, attending the Christmas vigil at St Mar-
tinès Abbey, the boy was seized with violent headaches which abated
only when he became a canon of St Martin. Fulk of Anjou provided
him with a canonical prebend and a hermitage near the abbey where
he adopted a life of asceticism, poverty, and prayer maintaining
nightly vigils at the tomb of the saint. His fellow hermit, Adheg-
rinus, led him to Baume, and after Abbot Berno's death he succeeded
him as abbot of Cluny.[27] He was eager to undertake monastic reforms
with the aid of bishops and pious lay lords like Count Gerald of
Aurillac, whom Odo presented to lay aristocrats of his day as a
model. On one of his reform ventures to Fleury, Odo was accompanied
by an armed contingent of counts and bishops, but he entered alone,
prevailing on the reluctant monks to accept his direction.[28]

It was at the very end of his life that Odo, at the behest of
Archbishop Teotolo, turned his attention to the restoration of monastic life at St Julien's Abbey. Lying at death's door in Italy, the
abbot prayed for the strength to return to his homeland and patron,
St Martin. His health was restored sufficiently for him to return
for the consecration of the new abbey on the Feast of St Martin,
11 November 942.[29] One can imagine a magnificent reunion of Teotolo, Odo, and the many lay and ecclesiastical supporters of St Julien,
some of whom had become the first monks. The saint spent his last
days composing for the feast a hymn which stressed the unity with
Christ and St Martin of all those who had contributed to the new
foundation. It reads in part:

> Thronging from all directions
> Enthusiastic people of all languages and races celebrate him,
> Vying with each other to rush to his tomb.
> Martin is highly deserving of such honor.
>
> This day fills the heavens and earth with Martin.
> May health come through you to those to whom you are famous.
> It is right, therefore, to rejoice; it is for the good of all,
> In the deeds done through you, worthy father.
>
> You restore peace here and immigrating to heaven,
> You have become our mediator with the Lord.
> This work is composed by Odo, your servant
> Emigrating from this world.

have mercy on us, Lord, whom you have nourished,
Ever merciful, most merciful one.
On your servant, Theotolo, and on all the others,
Have mercy, O Martin.[30]

St Julien became a symbol of spiritual renewal in the Touraine.
In place of the humble cell of the young St Odo, a reformed monastery of benedictine monks drawn from and supported by the aristocracy and people of the Touraine, glorified St Martin in their name.
St Odo chose to be buried among his new monks of St Julien.[31]

Monastic Reform by the Counts of Tours:
St Florent, Marmoutier, and Bourgueil

St Florent was established by Counts Tetbald of Blois and Tours
and Fulk the Good of Anjou before the outbreak of hostilities between
these neighboring provinces. In 958 a council of lay and ecclesiastical lords from Anjou, Touraine, and Brittany was convened to establish a new home at Saumur for the displaced monks of Montglonne near
Nantes and their relics of St Florent. St Florent was to be a symbol of peace on the borders of these provinces. Amalbertus, Abbot
of Fleury, was to establish benedictine life at the new abbey.[32]

Archbishop Arduin and his cathedral canons were the most generous donors to St Florent, but there were lay supporters as well.
In 960 a woman named Aremburgis gave a substantial allod.[33] A decade
later, Count Tetbald gave lands of the monastery of St Loup which he
had inherited from his parents.[34] In what was becoming typical of
the complicated exchanges and landholding arrangements of the late
tenth century, Guandalbertus, a nephew of the archbishop, requested
in 974 that his uncle Arduin grant St Florent a piece of arable land
of the Abbey of St Maximus, Chinon. Guandalbertus had originally
given this land to his brother, Rainaldus, who was to continue to receive a rent from the monks of St Florent. Thus laypersons, by prevailing on relatives in high ecclesiastical office, were not only
able to grant monasteries ecclesiastical lands, but maintain a continuing claim on them themselves.[35]

The peace of St Florent was soon encroached upon by both the
counts of Anjou and the castellans of Saumur. As early as 969,
Archbishop Arduin offered the monks of St Florent a house of refuge
and a prebend within the cloister of the cathedral.[36] They were
subject to frequent harassment, especially after 990, when Fulk of
Anjou began his attacks on the castle of Saumur.[37] The monastery
and castellan, Gelduin of Saumur, continuously disputed judicial
rights within the town. Gelduin had the right to try high crimes,
but by 978 he had usurped judicial rights over certain cases of
homicide, taxes and tolls which Count Tetbald had granted to the
monks. Count Odo threatened to concede the castle to another

fidelis unless the monks' rights were respected, and in 987 Gelduin
and Abbot Robert agreed to split any fee arising from adjudications
among merchants in the market at Saumur.[38]   A monastery like St Florent, established by the count, was proving an excellent check on the
power of a castellan guarding the count's borders.

At Marmoutier **benedictine** reform was ordered about 987 by Count
Odo of Tours, who called **upon** Abbot Mayolus of Cluny and some of his
monks to restore monastic life there.   There had been secular canons
of St Martin at Marmoutier for about a century, since a massacre of
monks by the Vikings.[39]   A story, which may contain some truth, cre-
dits the reform to Countess Bertha, wife of Odo of Tours and Blois;
she decided to attend services at Marmoutier one day while passing
by along the Loire, and discovered in residence only the canons'
wives ringing the bell for office with their children in their arms.
Incensed at the canons' neglect of duty, Bertha convinced her husband to appeal to the lay abbot of Marmoutier, Hugh Capet, to expel
the secular canons in favor of monks.[40]   When Abbot Majolus returned
to Cluny, a conflict ensued between the newly elected Abbot Berneri-
us of Marmoutier and some of the canons who had remained there as
monks.[41]   This struggle will be analyzed in a subsequent study of
secular canons and the Cluniac reform movement in the Touraine. Archbishop Arduin seems to have favored the canons, and one of his nephews did penance for invading the cloister and killing a cleric there,
perhaps in an effort to expel the **cluniacs**.[42]   Arduin, who was **trea-**
surer of Marmoutier, had alienated to his relatives and *fideles* some
of its property as well of lands of St Julien.   His death in the
midst of the controversy allowed Count Odo and his wife to succeed
in imposing monks at Marmoutier and to regain lands which they saw
slipping into the Archbishop's family's hands.[43]

With the election of Gauzbert, a relative of Count Odo, as abbot of Marmoutier, peace was restored and the recalcitrant canons
either left or adopted benedictine life.   The election of Gauzbert,
already abbot of St Julien and likewise abbot of Bourgueil, marked
a consolidation of the cluniac reform in the Touraine.   A kinsman
of this multiple abbot, Count Odo, has been accused of gaining control of monasteries as a part of a political consolidation program
in the Touraine.[44]

About 986, Count Odo returned to the monks he had recently established at Marmoutier a villa which had been unjustly alienated
from the abbey.[45]   A knight named Tetbald granted the monks an allod,
near the castle later known as Ile-Bouchard, land on which would
later be established the priory of Tavant.[46]   Harduin, the knight
who had killed a clerk in the cloister, gave the monks part of an
island in the Loire near his castle of Roches.[47]   In 991 the new
archbishop, Archembald, allowed his vassal, (and probable relative)
Robert, to exchange with the monks a **meadow** for vineyards and a mill
for a winepress.[48]   In 999 Corbo and his *fideles* Sulio gave Marmoutier

a meadow and a dam on the Choisille River.[49]

   A struggle between aristocratic families for control of Marmoutier may well be reflected in the charters of the last decade
of the tenth century. While Arduin remained archbishop and treasurer of the secular canons of Marmoutier, the Corbo-Arduins dis-
posed of the lands of this abbey which adjoined their castle of
Roches. With the monastic reform, Count Odo, Archbishop Archembald, and Abbot Gauzbert, who may all have been kinsmen, became the
dominant influences.[50] At Marmoutier, as at St Florent, the count
may have used the benedictine reform to strengthen his authority
in the bailliwick of an independent castellan. The power of Gelduin of Saumur was limited by the establishment there of the monastery of St Florent, and the power of the Corbo-Arduins by the monastic reform of Marmoutier. That the Corbo-Arduin and Gelduin families were formidable rivals to the counts of Tours is rendered
more creditable by the likelihood that they were part of one large
clan.[51] After the death of Count Odo and Hugh Capet and the succes-
sion of King Robert, whose father had been lay abbot of Marmoutier
before the reform, Robert took a renewed interest in the abbey and
city of Tours. He married Bertha, Odo's widow, until the marriage
was annulled by the pope under pressure from Count Fulk of Anjou.
King Robert, Queen Bertha, and the new young Count Odo all made donations to the monks of Marmoutier near the turn of the century.
The royal protection of Tours and armed resistance to invasion by
Fulk of Anjou on the part of the vicount and the citizens of Tours
averted the conquest of the Touraine by Fulk at the death of Count
Odo in 996.[52]

   Emma, the sister of Count Odo of Tours and wife of Count William of Aquitaine, founded Bourgueil in 990 on lands near Chinon
she had been given as a dowry. She may have been estranged from
William at the time of the foundation, but both her husband and her
brother Odo confirmed the foundation in 994. Odo also appointed
their relative Gauzbert then a monk of St Julien, as the first abbot of Bourgueil. This occurred several years before he became abbot of St Julien and then of Marmoutier. Gauzbert may have drafted
for Bourgueil the foundation charter which stressed the counts' responsibility for carrying on the work of the apostles in countering
'the evil tendencies of men to undermine the foundations or to sink
the ship of church on which they depend for salvation.' Bourgueil
was explicitly to follow the benedictine Rule.[53] It was a venture
of cooperation between the counts of Tours and Poitou, just as St
Florent, years earlier, had tried, unseccessfully, to cement relations between Anjou and Touraine.

   Various relatives of Emma's family made donations to the new
foundation. Archbishop Archembald and his *fidelis*, Corbo, and
Count Fulk of Anjou and his *fidelis*, Rainaldus, gave lands.[54] Hubert, knight of Saumur, sold the rights of justice at the castle

of Chinon to the monks of Bourgueil and made other donations to the
monastery in the first decade of the eleventh century.[55] At an un-
determined date the monks protested the depredations of the castellans of Mirebeau.[56] Bourgueil was caught in the mounting offensive
which was launched on the Touraine by Fulk and Geoffrey of Anjou and
which culminated in the capture of the Touraine by Geoffrey Martel
in 1044.

The Monastic Foundations of Herveus, Treasurer of St Martin: Beaumont, and St Côme

The life of the Blessed Herveus, treasurer of St Martin, parallels that of St Odo. He, too, was a hermit-canon of St Martin, and
founded two benedictine monasteries with the support of the local
aristocracy of Tours. Herveus may have been related to the Erkembald-Robert family, lords of Amboise and Buzançais, connected with
the founding of St Julien, and to Count Odo and Gilduin of Saumur.
He attended school at Fleury, but his family would not permit him
to become a monk there. King Robert offered him a prebend and later
the office of treasurer of St Martin, where, still desiring to live
as a monk, he adopted the canonical habit. He devoted his inheritance and **raised** money to rebuild the church of St Martin, which
had burned in the mid-990s. His favorite hermitage was on the island of St Côme, east of the city, which may have been the site of
St Odo's cell as well.[57]
Herveus moved closer to St Martin's Abbey as his responsibilities increased, and he turned St Côme over to monks of Marmoutier
to provide a retreat for those desiring greater solitude. Some
canons may have lived there with the monks, for a fragment dating
from this time of 'Rules of the Canons of Tours When They Live
in Common' has survived. Herveus was assisted by Count Odo
and his *fidelis*, Gelduin of Saumur, who donated the island to the
new foundation.[58]
Herveus befriended a group of women who were living a religious
life around the abbey of St Martin and attending the liturgical offices there. The **pope** had earlier **excluded** women from the abbey except for purposes of prayer. There had been no women's monastery in
the Touraine since the closing of St Loup in the mid-tenth century.
Herveus and other canons of St Martin donated family and ecclesiastical lands to the women. Prominent among lands given to the sisters
were lands of Ile-Bouchard. Herveus exchanged lands with a certain Eblo to get the original endowment, and Aimericus of the Castle
called Ile sold the nuns a villa for the substantial sum of one hundred *solidi*. These and other gifts were confirmed by Counts Odo and
Tetbald and by King Robert.[59]

Foundations by Local Aristocrats of the Touraine: Preuilly, Tavant, and Noyers

Viscount Atto of Tours in 937 traded lands with Hugh the Great, acting in his capacity of lay abbot of St Martin. Atto gave up his lands at Tours to the Abbey of St Martin and lost the office of viscount to Tetbald of Blois, who later became count. In exchange for his lands at Tours, Hugh the Great gave him at Preuilly, in the south of the Touraine, lands belonging to St Martin's Abbey. There Atto had already constructed a castle.[60] Atto's successor, Acfredus, used some of these lands in 1008 to endow the new monastery of Preuilly which he had built. His wife, Beatrix d'Issoudun, added lands from her inheritance in Berry. The new abbot, Amblard, drawn from Maillezais in Poitou, immediately borrowed five hundred Poitevin *solidi* from the lord of Preuilly, Gosbert, who had evidently succeeded his father, along with two ounces of gold to finance a trip to the Holy Land. Against his safe return of the money, he pledged a forest belonging to the monks.[61]

Three brothers may have been behind the foundation of three early eleventh-century monasteries. In 987 Tetbald gave to Marmoutier land which would be used for the foundation of the monastery of Tavant. His brother, Aimericus of the castle of Ile, contributed substantially to the women's monastery of Beaumont. Acfredus, the founder of Preuilly, was the third brother.[62] In 1020 Bouchard, now calling himself Knight and Lord of Ile-Bouchard, confirmed the endowment of the land given by his uncles to Marmoutier to the priory of Tavant.[63] Tavant was badly harassed in the wars between Anjou and Tours, and after 1044 Geoffrey Fuel, a nephew of Bouchard and a vassal of Geoffrey of Anjou, tried to claim lands of Tavant by force, but they were restored to the monks by another nephew of Bouchard.[64]

Just before the conquest of the Touraine by Anjou in 1044, the counts of Anjou became more prominent in monastic foundations in the Touraine. On the return from one of his pilgrimages to the Holy Land in 1007, Fulk of Anjou built the monastery of Holy Trinity, Beaulieu, on the model of the church of the Holy Sepulchre. He endowed it with extensive lands in the Touraine and the profits from the market at Loches.[65] Fulk and his wife were buried at Beaulieu and his son, Geoffrey, later added lands from St Ours, a priory which had been destroyed by the Vikings. Hugh, viscount of Chateaudun, who had succeeded Archembald as archbishop of Tours refused to consecrate the new abbey because of Fulk's recent ravaging of episcopal lands. A papal legate was, however, imported for the ceremony by the Count of Anjou.[66]

In 1030 Hubert of Noyant acquired the church of Noyers from Walrannus of Nouâtre, and with his son Thomas, a cleric, contributed a substantial endowment of lands for a new benedictine monastery

there. The land was held in benefice from Fulk and Geoffrey of Anjou, who gave their consent and more land.[67] Evrardus, already abbot of St Julien and Marmoutier, became the first abbot of Noyers
as well. He negotiated with Niva, lady of the castle of Faye, for
certain mill rights which were also claimed by a knight named Ebroinus, who raised an army and invaded the monastery. Abbot Evrardus
raised and led his own army of men who stood ready for war at the
Castle of Faye. Evrardus successfully held off the invaders until
Lady Niva arbitrated between him and Ebroinus and awarded the monks
two-thirds of the mill. For her support, the monks gave her one-
half ounce of gold. Among many other local aristocrats who contributed lands was Archembaldus, whose family may well have still held
the archbishopric of Tours.[68]

Conclusions

The first benedictine foundation in the Touraine in the tenth
century, that of St Julien, was initiated by Archbishop Teotolo and
his sister. That the many donations of the archbishop were approved by his lay and clerical *fideles*, illustrates the close cooperation in the benedictine movement of laity and clergy, drawn as they
were from the same aristocratic families.[69] Archbishop Arduin and
his family were deeply involved in several of the tenth-century
foundations and were particularly influential and substantial donors to St Julien, St Florent, Bourgueil and Marmoutier, before and
after its conversion to benedictine life.
In the late tenth century, Counts Tetbald and Odo, and Odo's
sister countess Emma of Poitou, provided the leadership for the new
foundations of St Florent and Bourgueil and for the reform of Marmoutier. Their families and *fideles*, especially Gelduin, castellan
of Saumur, and the Corbo-Arduins made generous gifts of land. Count
Fulk of Anjou, whose family had been active at Cormery during the
tenth century, founded Beaulieu in the early eleventh. In fact, the
counts of Anjou supported most of the monastic foundations in the
Touraine in this period. They were particularly active at St Juli-
en and St Florent in the early tenth century when Anjou and Touraine
were still at peace, and at Beaulieu and Noyers in the early eleventh century when Anjou was close to conquering the Touraine. Several
donors to these monasteries were characterized as *fideles* of the
counts of Anjou.
Beaumont and St Côme were the work of Herveus, treasurer of St
Martin, who may have been related to the Erkembald-Robert family,
later lords of Amboise and Buzançais. Gelduin of Saumur and Aimericus of Ile donated the first lands. This same Aimericus and his
brothers, Tetbald of Ile and Acfred of Preuilly, with their nephew,
Bouchard, lord of Ile, supported the foundation of Beaumont. Acfred
and his wife also founded the abbey of Preuilly. **Hubert** of Noyant,

Malrannus and Marricus of Noâtre, Niva, lady of Faye, and the ubiqui-
tous Archembaldus were major donors of land to Noyers.
 The aristocracy of the Touraine was drawn into the support of
benedictine houses by the archbishops and counts of Tours and Anjou,
who in the tenth century had the resources to initiate new foundations.
By the early eleventh century, however, certain venerable families of
the Touraine--the Erkembald-Roberts, the Corbo-Arduins, the Gelduins,
Tetbald-Bouchards, Atto-Acfreds and a few others--had become major
supporters of older monasteries and were founding new benedictine
houses of their own. It is no coincidence that these were also the
families who aspired to serve as castellans for the counts and even
lords of their own castles in the Touraine. Tenth-century monasteries like St Florent and Bourgueil had been built as sentinels on the
borders of the Touraine, spiritual defenses against chaos holding the
border from enemy attack no less effectively than did the castles of
Saumur and Chinon. As aristocrats became knights, castellans, and
lords by the year 1000, and as they became caught between the counts
of Tours-Blois and Anjou in the war over Tours, they too aspired to
introduce peace and stability to their lands through the spiritual
defenses of a resident community of benedictine monks.

Wheaton College
Norton, Massachusetts

NOTES

Abbreviations used in the article:

MSAT   *Memoires de la société archéologique de Touraine*
GC   *Gallia Christiana*
BEC   *Bibliothèque de l'école de chartes*
BSAT   *Bulletin trimestriel de la société archéologique*
              de Touraine
CCM   *Cahiers de Civilisation médiévale*
JS   *Journal des savants*
RM   *Revue Mabillon*
MS. BNTA   *Manuscript Bibliothèque nationale*, collection Touraine-
              Anjou (sometimes cited as collection Dom Housseau)
RB   *Revue Bénédictine*
TA   Martène and Durand, *Thesaurus novus anecdotorum*
PL   F.-P. Migne, *Patrologia latina*
RHGF   L. Deslisle, ed., Recueil des historiens des Gaules et de
              la France

1. Dom Gerald Sitwell, ed., trans., *St Odo of Cluny by John of
   Salerno and the Life of St Gerald of Aurillac by St Odo* (London,
   1958) 162.

2. Jean J. Bourassé, ed., *Cartulaire de Cormery precédé de l'histoire
   de l'abbaye et de la ville de Cormery d'après les chartes*, (Memoires de la société archéologique de Tourain, 12, 1861) xxxiv;
   B. Hauréau, ed., *Gallia Christiana*, 14 (Paris, 1856) 63-64; A. Salmon, 'Notice sur l'abbaye de Saint-Loup près de Tours,' *Bibliothèque de l'école de chartes*, 6 (1845) 436-453.

3. GC 14:63-64; Guy Oury, 'La situation juridique des monastères
   de Cormery et de Villeloin sous l'abbatiat de Guy d'Anjou' *BSAT*,
   37 (1975) 551-564.

4. Emile Mabille, *Les invasions normandes dans la Loire et les
   pérégrinations du corps de Saint-Martin* (Paris, 1869) 26; Edmond Martène and Casimir Chevalier, *Histoire de Marmoutier* (MSAT,
   24 [1874]) 1:177.

5. Jan Dhondt, *Études sur la naissance des principautés territori-
   ales en France*, IXe-X^e *siecles* (Bruges, 1948); Jacques Boussard,
   'Les destinées de la Neustrie du IXe au XIe siècle,' *Cahiers de
   civilisation médiévale*, 11 (1968) 15-28; J. Boussard, 'Les évêques
   en Neustrie avant la reforme gregorienne,' *Journal des savants*
   (1970)161-196; J. Boussard, 'Les origine des familles seigneuri-
   ales dans la région de la Loire moyenne,' *Cahiers de civilisation
   médiévale*, 5 (1962) 303-322; Karl F. Werner, 'Untersuchungen zur
   Frühzeit des franzosischen Fürstentums 9.-10. Jahrhundert,' *Die
   Welt als Geschichte*, 19 (1959) 168-190.

6. Friedrich Prinz, *Frühes Mönchtum im Frankenreich, Kultur und
   Gesellschaft in Gallien, den Rheinlanden und Bayern am Beispiel*

der monastischen Entwicklung (4. bis 8. Jahrhundert) (Munich, 1965); Guy Oury, 'L'éremitisme à Marmoutier,' *Bulletin de la société archéologique de Touraine*, 23 (1963) 319-334; G. Oury, 'Recherches sur les anciens monastères de la Touraine meridionale,' *Revue Mabillon* 55 (1965) 97-119; idem., 'Recherches sur quelques monastères nonidentifiés de la Touraine septentrionale,' *Revue Mabillon*, 53 (1963) 41-58; idem., 'L'éretisme dans l'ancien diocese de Tours au XIIe siècle,' *Revue Mabillon* 60 (1970) 43-90; Guy Devailly, 'Expansion et diversité du monachisme du Xe à XIe siècle,' *Histoire religieuse de la Touraine: Hommage à Christian Cury*, ed. Guy Oury (Tours, 1975) 51-73. See notes 2-3 regarding Cormery and Villeloin.

7. See below pp. 82-85.
8. See below pp. 85-88.
9. See below p. 88.
10. See pp. 89-90.
11. Guy Oury, 'La reconstruction monastique dans l'ouest: l'abbé Gauzbert de Saint-Julien de Tours,' *Revue Mabillon*, 54 (1964) 118-123.
12. Charles de Grandmaison, ed., *Fragments de chartes du Xe siècle provenant de Saint-Julien de Tours* (Paris, 1886) nos. V-VIII, 24-28.
13. Jean Mabillon, ed., *Vetera analecta* (Paris, 1723) 3:657. Grandmaison, *Fragments*, no. XXI, 57-60; Joseph Delaville le Roulx, *Notices sur les chartes originales relatives à la Touraine antérieures à l'an mil* (Tours, 1879) nos. XV-XVI, 39-43; mss. Bibliothèque nationale, collection Touraine-Anjou, I, nos. 154 and 167; Werner, *Die Welt als Geschichte*, 19 (1959) 179; Emile Mabille, *La pancarte noire de Saint-Martin de Tours*, MSAT, 17 (1867) no. X. Boussard, CCM 5 (1962) 314. For Herveus see note 57 below.
14. Grandmaison, *Fragments*, no. III, 19-21.
15. *Ibid.*, no. XV, 48-50.
16. *Ibid.*, no. XIX, 54-56 and no. XVIII, 53-54.
17. Prosper Tarbé, 'Examen critique et analytique de diverses chartes de X^e, XIe, XIIe, siècles relatives à la Touraine,' *Revue retrospective* 9 (1837) 32-35; Grandmaison, *Fragments* no. XXVI, 69-71.
18. Grandmaison, *Fragments*, nos. IV, XXII, XXVII, XXVIII and XXX, pp. 21-24, 60-62, 71-73, 82-84; Tarbé, *Revue retrospective* 9:35-37.
19. Grandmaison, *Fragments*, nos. VII-VIII, 29-38.
20. Delaville le Roulx, *Notices*, no. XVI, 41-43.
21. *Ibid.* no. XIII, pp. 29-31; Werner, *Die Welt als Geschichte* 19: 173-175; mss. BNTA, I, no. 166; Grandmaison, *Fragments*, nos. IV and X, 21-24 and 40-42; André Salmon, *Le livre de serfs de Marmoutier* (MSAT, XVI, 1864) no. LXII, 68-70.
22. Delaville le Roulx, *Notices*, no. XV, 39-41.

23. See note 18 above.
24. Madeleine Dillay, 'Le régime de l'église privée du XIe au XIIIe siècle dans l'Anjou, le Maine et la Touraine: les restitutions d'églises par les laïques,' *Revue historique de droit francaise et étranger* 4 (1925) 253-294; Bernard Chevalier, 'Les restitutions d'église dans le diocese de Tours du Xe au XIIe siècles,' *Études de civilisation médiévale: Melanges offerts à Edmond-Rêné Labande* (Poitiers, 1974) 129-143.
25. Guy Oury, *Revue Mabillon* 54 (1964) 69-124.
26. G. Sitwell, *St Odo of Cluny by John of Salerno*, p. 8, note 1, observes that an *Abbo legislator*, appearing in an 898 document of Tours, may have been Odo's father, according to Ernst Sackur, *Die Cluniacenser in ihrer kirchlichen und allgemeingeschichtlichen Wirksamkeit bis sur mitte des elften Anjou Jahrhunderts* (Halle, 1892) I, 44, note 4; however, see J. Wollasch, 'Königtum, Adel und Klöster in Berry während des 10. Jahrhunderts,' *Neue Forschungen über Cluny und die Cluniacenser*. ed., J. Wollasch, Hans E. Mager, and H. Diener (Freiburg, 1959) 54-56, 68-82, 125-128, 134-141.
27. G. Sitwell, *St Odo of Cluny by John of Salerno*, 6-16, 19-20, 24-27, 31-35, 39-41.
28. *Ibid.*, 79-81, and Sitwell, *St Odo of Cluny, Life of St Gerald of Aurillac*, 90-180.
29. *St Odo of Cluny*, 85-87, and Mabillon, *Vetera analecta*, 3:659.
30. *Ibid.*, Instinctu supero cardine quadrifido
     Gens, linguae, populi hunc celebrant seduli,
     Certatimque fluit illius ad tumulum:
     Martinum decet hoc decus.

     Haec Martine dies arva polosque replet,
     Sit per te salubris, his quibus est celebris.
     Sit gaudere pium, sit generale bonum,
     Hoc per te pater inclite.

     Tu pacem reparas: hic & ad astra migrans,
     Nunc nos te medio concilies Domino,
     Odonis famuli hoc opus qui condidit
     Emigrans de saeculo.

     Misertus Domine, quos enutristi pie
     Semper misericors, misericordissime,
     Tetolonis servi ceterisque tuis
     Miserere, O Martine.
31. Oury, *Revue Mabillon* 54 (1964) 123; Kassius Hallinger, 'The Spiritual Life of Cluny in the Early Days,' in Noreen Hunt (ed.), *Cluniac Monasticism in the Central Middle Ages* (Hamden, CT, 1971) 32-43.

32. Étienne Baluze, *Histoire généalogique de la maison d'Auvergne*
(Paris, 1708) II, 23; Maurice Hamon, 'La vie de Saint-Florent
et les origines de l'abbaye du Mont-Glonne,' *Bibliothèque de
l'école de chartes* 129 (1971) 215-238; 'Historia sancti Flor-
entii Salmurensis,' in Paul Marchegay and Emile Mabille, *Chroniques des églises d'Anjou* (Paris, 1869) 2:231-264.
33. Robert Latouche, *Histoire du comté du Maine pendant le Xe et
le XIe siècle* (Paris, 1910) Pièces justificatives no. 1, 161-
162.
34. Edmond Martène, ed. *Thesaurus novus anecdotorum,* (Paris, 1717)
1:91-92, and mss. Bibliothèque nationale, collection Touraine-
Anjou, I, no. 176.
35. Archbishop Arduin and his canons made the following gifts: mss.
Bibliothèque nationale, collection Touraine-Anjou, I, nos. 190,
194, 197, 199, 195, 200, 196, 200*bis*; Martène, *Thesaurus* 1:90;
Guandalbertus' gift may be found in mss. BN, Touraine-Anjou I,
no. 217; St Maximus, Chinon, was restored to monastic occupation
in 938 by Archbishop Teotolo as a priory of St Julien. This
foundation will be examined in a subsequent paper on canons and
monastic reform; the charter may be found in Philippe Lauer,
Actes de Louis d'Outremer (Paris, 1914) *Revue Mabillon* 54: no.
41 as noted by Oury, RM 54:122.
36. For the politics surrounding the establishment of St Florent, see
Bernard Bachrach, 'Robert of Blois Abbot of Saint-Florent de
Saumur and Saint-Mesmin de Micy (985-1011) a Study in Small Power Politics,' *Revue Bénédictine* 88 (1978) 123-146; Martène,
Thesaurus 1:90.
37. Bachrach, RB 88:130; J. M. Bienvenu, 'Pauvreté, misères et charité
en Anjou aux XIe et XIIe siècles,' *Le Moyen age,* 72 (1966) 403.
38. Bachrach, RB 88:130-131; Martène, TA 1:94-95; Gustave D'Espinay,
ed. *Les cartulaires angevins: étude sur le droit d'Anjou au moy-
en âge* (Angers, 1864) 325-326.
39. See note 4 above for the Viking massacre and establishment of
canons at Marmoutier; André Salmon, ed., *Recueil de chroniques
de Touraine* (Tours, 1854, 1856) 309-314 and 355-359; Martène
and Chevalier, *Marmoutier,* 1:200-234; a charter of 980 to 990
alludes to the reform: mss. BN Touraine-Anjou, II/1, no. 281:
'ad locum Sancti Martini quod dicitur Majus Monasterium...unde
venerabilis vir Majolus abbas esse videtur.'
40. Salmon, *Chroniques de Touraine,* 309-314; 355-359; Martène and
Chevalier, *Marmoutier,* 1:200-234; Sackur, *Die Cluniacenser*
245-246.
41. Abbo of Fleury, Letters; PL 139:429-433.
42. Ms. BN Touraine-Anjou, I, 228.
43. Pierre Lévêque, 'Trois actes faux ou interpolés des Comtes Eudes
et Robert et du Roi Raoul en faveur de l'abbaye de Marmoutier,
887, 912, 931,' BEC, 64 (1903) 54-82, 289-305; Richer, *Histoire*

de France, 888-995, ed. Robert Latouche, (Paris, 1937) 1:308;
Adémar de Chabannes, *Chronique*, ed. J. Chavanon (Paris, 1897)
34; Pierre Imbart de la Tour, *Les élections épiscopales dans
l'église de France du IXe au XIIe siècle* (Paris, 1891) 242-244.

44. The charters which trace the transition from canons to monks
    at Marmoutier may be found in the mss. BN, **Touraine-Anjou**, I,
    nos. 231, 232 & 233; II/1, no. 281; B. Haureau, ed., *Gallia
    Christiana* 14:62; Count Odo's political motives for the reform
    are analysed by Lévèque, BEC, 64 (1903) 54-82 and 289-305.

45. Ms. BNTA, I, no. 231.

46. A. de Martonne, 'Charte de fondation du prieuré de Tavant,'
    BEC 19, ser. 4 (1858) 362-368.

47. Ms. BNTA, I, no. 228.

48. Delaville le Roulx, *Notices*, no. XII, 27-29.

49. Ms. BNTA, II/1, no. 283.

50. Werner, *Die Welt als Geschichte* 19:179; J. Boussard, JS (1970)
    161-196 and CCM, 5 (1962) 302-322, does not link Archbishop
    Archembald (of Sully?) with the local Erkembald-Roberts, but
    I am inclined to think he does belong to this prominent family
    of the Touraine, who often held the archbishopric. The rela-
    tion of a Gauzbert to the Erkembald-Robert family is shown
    in Mabille, *La pancarte noire*, no. X (954).

51. Boussard, CCM, 5 (1962) 314.

52. Richer, *Histoire*, 1:308; Adhémar de Chabannes, *Chronique*, 34
    discuss the marriage alliance; Salmon, ed., *Chroniques de Tour-
    aine*, 228 and ms. BNTA, II/1, no. 275 refer to Bertha as queen;
    Luc D'Achery, E. Baluze and E. Martène, *Spicilegium sive collec-
    tio veterum aliquot scriptorum* (Paris, 1723) 1:602-603 records
    the excummunications over the marriage; see Olivier Guillot, *Le
    comté d'Anjou et son entourage au XIe siècle* (Paris, 1972) 1:
    24-26 and Louis Halphen, *Le comté d'Anjou au XIe siècle* (Paris,
    1906) 32, for the repudiation and remarriage. For the invasion
    of Tours by Fulk and the resistance of the citizens, see Richer,
    Histoire, I, 278-283; Adhémar de Chabannes, *Chronique*, 34; Sal-
    mon, *Chroniques de Touraine*, 228; for the gifts to Marmoutier
    mss, BNTA, nos 275, 276 and 334. Count Odo's son Tetbald ruled
    as count from 996-1004 when he was succeeded by his brother Odo
    II, see Bachrach, RB 88 (1978) 134.

53. Delaville le Roulx, *Notices*, 31-38; Michel Dupont, *Monographie
    du cartulaire de Bourgueil des origines a la fin du moyen age*,
    (Tours, MSAT, 56, 1962) 161-162; PL 146:1247-1272; Oury, RM 54
    (1964) 77-84.

54. Mss. BNTA, II/1, nos. 270, 282; Delaville le Roulx, *Notices*, 31-
    41; Tarbé, *Revue retrospective*, 9 (1837) 46-55.

55. Dupont, *Bourgueil*, 167-169.

56. Tarbé, *Revue retrospective*, 9 (1837) 48-49.

57. Richer, *Histoire*, 1:278-9; Salmon, *Chroniques de Touraine*, 51,

229, 301; 'Vita Hervei' in Martène, *Thesaurus*, 3:1349-1350;
Oury, RM, 54 (1964) 120; Mabillon, *Vetera Analecta*, 4:695;
Jacques Boussard, 'Le tresorier de Saint-Martin de Tours,'
Revue d'histoire d'église de France, 47 (1961) 61-81; Guy
Oury, 'L'ideal monastique dans la vie canoniale: le Bienheureux
Hervé de Tours,' 50 (1960) 1-29.

58. *Ibid.*, and 'Fragmentum statutorum canonicorum Turonensium cum
vivebant in communi,' in PL:138, cols. 1349-1350; Mabillon,
Vetera Analecta, 4:695, is the charter of foundation.

59. A. Salmon, 'Notice sur l'abbaye de Saint-Loup près de Tours,'
BEC, VI (1845) 436-453; Tarbé, *Revue retrospective*, 9 (1837)
26-29; for the Beaumont charters, RHGF, 10:589 and 607; Mabillon
Annales ordinis Sancti Benedicti, 4:696-7 and 708; ms. BNTA,
II/1, nos. 273, 322, 376, 377.

60. Ms. BNTA, I, no. 166; Boussard, CCM. 5 (1962) 322.

61. RHGF, 10, 600; mss. BNTA, I, nos. 342, 343, 339 and 386.

62. See notes 46, 59 and 61 for relevant charters.

63. GC, 14, 194 or Martonne, BEC, 19, ser. 4, 365, for the 987
grant and BNTA, II/1, no. 373 for the 1020 confirmation.

64. MS. BNTA, II/1, nos. 450 and 533; Jacques Boussard, 'L'eviction
des tenants de Thibaud de Blois par Geoffroi Martel, comté
d'Anjou en 1044,' *Le moyen age*, 69 (1963) 141-149.

65. Halphen, *Comté d'Anjou*, 83-6, 351-2 (authentic charter) and
219-31 (*re* false charters in GC, 14 Instr. col. 64-6 and ms.
BNTA, II/1, nos. 337 and 357); Guillot, *Comté d'Anjou*, I, 127;
II, 59-60, and 275.

66. *Ibid.* Archambald (before 987 to after 1006) and Hugh of Chateaudun (before 1007 to 1023); Oury, *Histoire religieuse de Touraine*,
308.

67. Casimir, Chevalier, ed., *Histoire de l'abbaye de Noyers au XIe
et au XIIe siècle d'après les chartes*, (Tours, MSAT, 23, 1873)
nos. 1 and 3, pp. 1-3 and 4-6.

68. *Ibid.*, no. 2, 3-4, and no. 4, p. 6 and nos. 6-8, pp. 7-12;
BNTA, II/1 no. 468.

69. See the charters of St Julien cited in note 12.

Benedictine Monasteries in the Touraine 930-1030

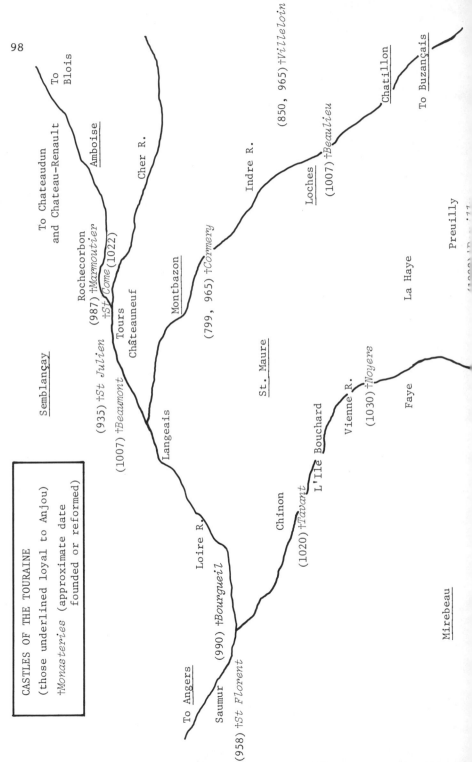

CASTLES OF THE TOURAINE
(those underlined loyal to Anjou)
†*Monasteries* (approximate date
founded or reformed)

To Chateaudun
and Chateau-Renault

Semblançay

Amboise

Cher R.

Rochecorbon
(987) †*Marmoutier*
†*St Côme* (1022)

(935) †*St Julien*

Tours

Châteauneuf

(1007) †*Beaumont*

Montbazon

(799, 965) †*Cormery*

Indre R.

(850, 965) †*Villeloin*

Loches

(1007) †*Beaulieu*

Chatillon

To Buzançais

Langeais

St. Maure

La Haye

Preuilly

Loire R.

Chinon

(1020) †*Tavant*

L'Île Bouchard

Vienne R.

(1030) †*Noyers*

Faye

To Angers

Saumur (990) †*Bourgueil*

(958) †*St Florent*

Mirebeau

THE *CONVERSUS* OF CLUNY: WAS HE A LAY-BROTHER?

Cyprian Davis, O.S.B.

'The tenth degree of humility,' says the *Rule of St Benedict*,
'is that one not be easily given or quickly inclined to laughter;
for it is written: the stupid man raises his voice in laughter'
(RB 7). Our goal is not to examine the meaning of this passage
from St Benedict's treatise on humility, found in chapter seven of
the rule that bears his name. Nor do we want to talk about laughter
in a solemn assembly of scientific historical inquiry. In fact, what
we want to do is ask a question that has some bearing on monastic
life today. Was the monk known as a *conversus* in the monastery of
Cluny a lay-brother in our modern sense of the term? In order to
try to answer that question, I would like to begin with the case of
the laughing monk. It is important that he is laughing because he
caused others to laugh and that was precisely what he was not supposed to do. But had he not been a jokester, we would not have known
the name of a *conversus* at Cluny.

The author of the oldest life of St Hugh the Great, abbot at Cluny from 1049 to 1109, mentions the anecdote of this monk, who had to
pay the consequences for his jokes and laughter. The author is Gilo,
who became a cardinal and who supported Pope Anacletus II in opposition to St Bernard, who supported Pope Innocent II. Gilo's account
is like this:

> A certain brother, Durannus de Bredon by name, who was
> first known as an *idiota* and afterwards became not un-
> fittingly abbot of Moissac and then by the persuasive
> election of wisdom was elevated to the episcopal see of
> Toulouse...this Durannus was renowned among the workers
> in the fields of the Lord by his meritorious solicitude
> and labor. But he who was circumspect in all things was
> a little less careful in this...he brought forth words
> that moved others often injudiciously to laughter. As a
> result the venerable father, that is St Hugh, rebuked
> him many times.[1]

Gilo goes on to point out that when admonition had little effect on
Durannus, St Hugh foretold that the monk would be forced to appear
after his death with foaming lips. And in fact, this happened. Durannus appeared to one of the monks of Cluny who would later serve as
chaplain to Abbot Hugh and told him that he needed help in expiating
his sinful levity while on earth. Hugh the Great, informed of this,
came to Durannus' help by ordering seven monks to maintain absolute
silence for a week in reparation on Durannus' behalf. In point of

fact, one of the monks failed to keep silence and another week of
reparation by seven monks was needed. In the end, however, Durannus was freed from his period of suffering.

The important thing for us is not that Durannus could never re-
sist telling jokes--and we can imagine that they were slightly off-
color in the best Latin tradition--but that he is characterized as
being an *idiota*, a word that gives us our word 'idiot' but which in
medieval Latin meant one who could not read Latin. Durannus was an
idiota, but, as Gilo reminds us, not unfittingly did he become abbot
of the Cluniac abbey of Moissac near Toulouse, and thereafter bishop
of Toulouse in 1059. Durannus died in either 1072 or 1073. Though
an *idiota* and a *conversus* (as we shall see the terms were interchange-
able), he learned to read and he became first an abbot and then a
bishop.

Even more intriguing is the young man of whom John of Salerno
wrote in his life of St Odo, the first abbot of Cluny from 926 to
942--the first abbot, that is, after the death of St Berno, the founder of Cluny. John of Salerno accompanied St Odo on his many travels
as abbot. There is a certain frontier flavor of the American West in
a scene that John of Salerno witnessed as the saintly abbot and his
party made their way on horseback through dangerous territory.

> One day as [Odo] was making his way along an area border-
> ing on the hangout of robbers, a certain bandit, a young
> man, saw the kindness in Odo's face and was at once moved
> to heartfelt sorrow for his sins. Throwing himself at
> his feet, he begged with a humble voice that [Odo] would
> have mercy on him.
>
> When Odo asked him what he wanted, he requested that
> he be aided by the monastic mercy for himself. [Such a
> phrase was the ritual request for admission into the com-
> munity.] Then our father asked him if there was some one
> from the parish who might know him. [The young man] re-
> plied: Everyone does.[2]

John of Salerno goes on to say that St Odo directed the young man to
come back the next day with a noteworthy person from the parish who
might vouch for his character. John then describes how the young
man returned with a nobleman from the parish. Interrogated about
the young man, the nobleman revealed that the young man in question
was a notorious bandit. St Odo suggested to the young man that he
take some time for personal renewal before joining the monastery,
but when the young bandit protested that any delay would surely en-
danger his soul and that Odo would be held responsible, Odo--who was
always 'all heart'--accepted the young bandit into the community.
John of Salerno does not say that the community was Cluny--Odo already had charge of other monasteries--but it well could have been.

In recounting the later career of the erstwhile bandit, John
of Salerno wrote:

> When some little time had passed, he, living under the
> trial of the rule, was finally made a monk. They placed
> him under the authority of the cellarer for obedience.
> Moreover, since he was an *idiota*, they imposed upon him
> the dual task of obedience and the study of letters. This
> he carried out devotedly so that he reached out one hand
> to obedience and the other held the psalter.[3]

In fact, the newly converted monk was soon ripe for heaven, to which
the Blessed Virgin in a vision soon invited him according to John of
Salerno.

History is always the study of flesh and blood human beings.
The laughing monk with a good story on his lips and the converted
bandit who learned to read by means of the psalter tell us something
about the monastic population. In particular, Gilo and John of Salerno have told us something about those adults who entered the community late in life or more precisely after childhood or adolescence
and were therefore known as *idiotae* or *conversi*.

The *conversi* at Cluny are mentioned in the earliest customaries.
These texts containing the rules and directions for the celebration
of the liturgical seasons and feasts, the rules for the ceremonies
that were the framework of the monks' daily existence, first appeared at the beginning of the eleventh century. The first customaries
--there are three versions very similar in content-- only mention the
conversi in the context of the liturgy. Invariably they served as
acolytes, that is, they carried the candles and the censer. They also carried the processional cross during the frequent processions
that were already characteristic of the cluniac liturgy.

A customary that is slightly later in date but which also belongs
to the first third of the eleventh century is the so-called Customary
of Farfa, better referred to as the *Liber Tramitis*, the title given
to it in the splendid text in the Vatican Museum (Vat. Lat. 6808).[4]
To have some idea as to the rôle of the *conversi* at the liturgical
celebration of Easter in the time of St Odilo (994-1049) let us lis-
ten to this description of the preparation for the Conventual Mass
on Easter Sunday at Cluny:

> As soon as the water has been blessed, let them begin
> this antiphon, *Vidi Aquam*. Then two of the youths or
> children, whom the *armarius* will have chosen shall come
> forward. Then four priests shall arrive in turn taking
> the lesser relics. Let there be twelve *conversi* of whom
> four shall carry the candles and two shall be prepared

with the censer. Another shall carry the incense, four
others shall carry the crosses, and one the holy water.
Let the cantors begin the responsary of Blessed Mary as
they deem fitting. And thus they shall proceed in order:
in the first place the holy water, the cross, and the
priests....Then the two crosses and a crucifix in the
middle. Two candle bearers follow and one [monk] carrying the text [of the epistles] in the center. Likewise
two other candle bearers with [another monk] in the middle
carrying the Gospel book.[5]

The customary describes how the rest of the community follows. When
they arrived at the church, the sacristan handed a cope to each monk,
even to the *conversi,* and a tunic to the children. For Easter Sunday as for all the great feasts at Cluny the whole community of adult
monks wore copes and on other, slightly lesser feasts, albs. But almost always the text of the customaries adds the phrase *etiam ad con-
versos*. Thus it is that by the beginning of the eleventh century the
references to the *conversi* pertain for the most part to their function
in the liturgy at Cluny. In fact, their presence was indispensable
to the solemnity of the rites.

The customaries also indicate to us that the term *idiota* is a
synonym for *conversus* at Cluny. The *Liber Tramitis* (Customary of
Farfa) says that on the feast of St John the Baptist (24 June) at
the major conventual Mass 'all are to be clad in copes even the
idiote--all the youths, of course, in tunics.'[6] The same customary
has the same language to describe the vesture of the community on
August 1st, the Feast of St Peter in Chains, an important feast at
Cluny because St Peter was the **titular** patron of the abbey: 'At the
major conventual Mass all priests and deacons are in copes, also even
the *conversi* who know how to sing; the children shall have tunics.'[7]

Here too another important distinction is made: the *conversi* 'who
know how to sing.' More frequently the text reads 'who do not know
how to sing.' The variation in the text is important because it tells
us something else about the cluniac *conversus*. In a community where
liturgical ceremonies were the warp and woof of the daily fabric and
where both the singing of the psalmody as well as the intricate melodies of the antiphons and responsories were an essential **part** of the
Office and the numerous processions, the *conversi* were not prohibited
from singing.

In the more elaborate and detailed customaries of Bernard and
Ulrich which date from the last quarter of the eleventh century, there
is a more complete description of the duties and position of the *conversi*. They pour the wine at table, vested in amice and alb they as-
sist at the quasi-liturgical ceremony of baking the altar bread or
hosts, and they can be **raised by** the abbot to higher rank in seniority.
More surprisingly, the eleventh-century Bernard in his customary

also indicates that a *conversus* could serve as the guardian for a
youth in the community. Except in liturgical processions, when
youths being trained as monks walked with *cantores*, those who could
sing, a youth remained with his guardian who, if a *conversus*, did not
know how to sing.[8]

In fact, the make-up of the community at the end of the eleventh century is indicated to some extent by a rather banal detail,
namely the number of hand towels next to the fountain in the cloister. Each monastic sub-group had its respective towel. According
to Ulrich there were three: one for the youths, the second for those
who can sing, the third for the *idiote*.[9] Bernard stipulates that
there are five: two for the priests and deacons, one for the youths,
and two others for the *cantores* and the *conversi*.[10]

The *conversus* at Cluny in the eleventh century was a lay monk.
He is one who entered the monastic community as an adult and, as a
result, was very often unable to read—although many, like our converted bandit must have learned to do so. He did not know by heart
the elaborate melodies of the Mass and Office. As a result the *conversi* were in a different category from the monks who had lived from
childhood in the monastery. These are the men who are designated
conversi of the older type by historians since the time of Jean Mabillon.[11] In this way they are **distinguished from the** *conversi* **of the**
newer type or the modern lay-brother who is the *frater laicus* or *frater conversus* so important in reformed monasticism, particulary of
the Cistercians, in the twelfth century.

Many historians have believed that an evolution took place from
the one type to the other. Kassius Hallinger suggested in 1956 that
Cluny in the time of Peter the Venerable (1122-1156) was the place
where the missing link between the two types of *conversi* was to be
found.[12] He suggested that this *conversus* was the **bearded** *conversus*,
the *conversus barbatus* mentioned by Peter the Venerable in his famous
statutes drawn up in the years 1146-1156 as a response to St Bernard.

In a colorful passage, Peter indignantly complained about the
lay servants or *famuli* who listened to the **gossip** of the sick monks
and broadcast the news all over town and who helped themselves and
their families in town to the food given to the sick monks. Using
this behavior as a pretext, Peter replaced the *famuli* in the infirm-
ary with the *conversi*, whom he describes as being bearded. Giles
Constable in 1973 expressed the opinion that the phrase bearded *conversi* marked not a new institution but rather an insistence by Peter
the Venerable that the men be of mature age and experience. In the
same way a distinction was made between bearded *famuli* and beardless
famuli.[13] **The latter were not of mature age and therefore unfitted**
for certain positions. I agree with Giles Constable, mainly because
this particular statute of Peter the Venerable is in fact the only
place where the bearded *conversi* are mentioned. It would seem that
a new institution of bearded *conversi* would make their appearance

more than once in the cluniac documents.

On the other hand, it seems to me that a subtle change did occur in the status of the *conversi* at Cluny at this time. This gradual change in status resulted from a shift in attitude. The 'missing link' does not exist, but a mutation did occur. Another of the statutes of Peter the Venerable provides a clue.

In statute thirty-nine, Peter the Venerable orders a restoration of 'the ancient and holy manual labor,' and gives the following explanation:

> The reason for this institution has been that idleness,
> which according to our Father Benedict is the enemy of
> the soul, is the pasttime in great measure of our own
> men, especially of those who are called *conversi,* so
> that in the cloister or outside it, except for the few
> who read and even the more rare number who write, they
> either cling to the walls of the cloister, asleep; or
> from the rising of the sun to its setting, so to speak,
> --and even half the night, if they could do so--they con-
> sume nearly the whole day with vain, idle gossip, and
> what is worse, with words full of detraction.[14]

With this **measure** Peter the Venerable augmented the manual labor for the monks in general and **for the** *conversi* in particular, who by and large were illiterate. From that time on the statutes of various abbots promulgated for the entire Cluniac congregation began to associate manual labor with the *conversi*. In 1200, Abbot Hugh V promulgated a statute, which would be continually reiterated by subsequent abbots, curtailing the number of new recruits in the diverse cluniac houses because the economic resources were not increasing and a large number of monks could not be supported. Among certain exceptions, however, were those who would be received as *conversi* 'who as [such] are apt and necessary for agriculture or for the performance of other useful work.'[15] By this time the *conversus* was thought of in the Cluniac congregation in terms of manual labor. At the same time the statutes begin to mention monks and then *conversi* in series. Time does not permit the examination of each of these passages in turn. But we must ask whether this differentiation between monks and *conversi* does not indicate a shift in the meaning of *conversus*.

Perhaps the most telling sign of what might appear to be a *rapprochement* in status between the *conversus* of Cluny and the *conversus* at Cîteaux or any of the other reformed monastic orders occurs in the statutes of Abbot Bertrand I in 1301. In a series of statutes that relate specifically to the abbey of Cluny we find the following:

...let no one from the community of Cluny who follows
the convent and is present in the community dare or presume to sleep outside the dormitory without a special
permission form us or from our successors. Only those
are excepted to whom it has been permitted to sleep
outside of the dormitory for a just reason (either) in
the church, in the dormitory of the *conversi,* or in
some other place through ancient custom.[16]

One might remark facetiously that most monks sleep in church at one
time or another, but the text probably refers to the sacristan and
his assistant in quarters near the church. For us what is important
is that this text mentions for the first and the only time the dormitory of the *conversi*. The old customaries presume that all of the
monks, including the *conversi*, slept in the same large hall. A special dormitory for the *conversi* was a characteristic of the Cistercians and the other reformed monastic orders. Its appearance at
Cluny might seem to indicate in a conclusive way that the shift of
the *conversi* to lay-brothers was now complete. Yet such a dormitory
is not mentioned in any of the subsequent medieval statutes. It is
not mentioned even when it should be. As a result, one can only con-
clude that a dormitory of the *conversi* existed for a brief period
around 1301; or that it had existed for some time and continued to
exist but the early fourteenth century witnessed the new problem of
monks not sleeping where they should, which caused specific mention
to be made of the sleeping-place of the *conversi;* or finally that
the statutes of Abbot Bertrand I, extant in a fourteenth-century
copy, were touched up by later writers or copyists. In the face of
problems like this one is forced to realize that many details of
monastic life were so ordinary as to be taken for granted and left
unmentioned in the documents.

For this reason there remain many unanswered questions regarding the *conversi* both at Cluny itself and in the congregation at
large. What were the specific duties allotted the *conversi* in the
later Middle Ages? Only a few charters remain to indicate that at
Cluny itself the *conversi* had responsibilities relating to the do-
main itself. Nothing reveals their number, although there are indications from other Cluniac houses that with few exceptions the
number of *conversi* was always very small. The estates or deaneries
of Cluny were farmed by serfs. The grange with a work-force of
monks or laybrothers simply did not exist at Cluny. The *famuli* or
lay servants seem to have increased in size as the medieval period
progressed. Domestic help was never replaced by *conversi*.

This brings us back to our original question: was the medieval *conversus* at Cluny a lay-brother? My answer is no, he was not.
What is more, there is no incontrovertible evidence to show that
the *conversus* of Cluny ever evolved into the lay-brother or that

lay-brothers were ever introduced alongside the *conversi*. Finally,
there is nothing to indicate that the old type of *conversi* simply
died out and the newer type appeared. Such a drastic institutional
shift at a place like Cluny, where liturgical rank was all important,
would never have been allowed to go unnoticed in the documentation.
Nevertheless, the documents reveal that after 1200 a shift in understanding and appreciation did occur. Consciously and subconsciously
many of the elements typical of the cistercian lay-brother and even
of the lay-brothers of the mendicant orders began to be applied to
the Cluniac *conversus*, who had never been a lay-brother but had always been an integral member of the community--integral though often
subordinate, to be sure. By the thirteenth century the name had
shifted in meaning. Even though the juridical constitution of the
Cluniac *conversi* as lay-brothers in the modern sense did not occur
in the Middle Ages, the connotations of the new status filtered
through to the other.

Just such a shift in meaning has been going on in reverse in
benedictine houses since the Second Vatican Council. In most benedictine congregations the status of lay-brothers has changed until
today there exists only one class of monks in most monasteries. Effectively, the lay-brother has ceased to exist; for now he partici-
pates in chapter, sings the canonical hours in the vernacular with
the entire community, wears the cowl, walks according to seniority
regardless of sacred orders or the absence, and all new recruits
henceforth admitted to profession make solemn vows.

And yet in many monasteries tensions still exist. There are
priests, clerics, and brothers. The older mentality changes but
gradually. Sentiment has not kept pace with law. The social evolution of external society does not always move at the same tempo
as deeply held convictions regarding order and the meaning of vocation. Historians two centuries from now will have great difficulty
untangling the meaning of our categories in late twentieth-century
monasticism. It will be almost impossible for them to pin-point or
even precisely to trace the shifts of meaning in the terms still
used--'brother,' 'non-priest monk,' 'choir monk,' 'apprentice-monk.'
Perhaps the very proliferation of terms will indicate to them what
the same phenomenon indicated in the Middle Ages--an ongoing effort
to refine one's understanding of the monastic charism, a desire to
deepen one's perception of the monastic ideal.

St Meinrad's Archabbey
St Meinrad, Indiana

NOTES

1. *Vita* of St Hugh by Gilo, edited by A. L'Huillier, *Vie de Saint Hugues, Abbé de Cluny.* Solesmes, 1888. *Documents*, pp. 591-592.

2. *Vita Sancti Odonis,* by John of Salerno. *Bibliotheca Cluniacensis.* c. 49. PL 133, cc. 71-72.

3. *Ibid.*

4. A critical edition of the text has recently appeared, edited by Peter Dinter, *Liber Tramitis Aevi Odilonis Abbatis,* in the *Corpus Consuetudinum Monasticarum,* t. X. Siegburg, 1980.

5. *Ibid.,* p. 89.

6. *Ibid.,* p. 126.

7. *Ibid.,* p. 144.

8. Customary of Bernard, *Vetus Disciplina Monastica,* edited by M. Herrgott. Paris, 1726, p. 210ss.

9. Customary of Ulrich, PL 149, c. 706.

10. Customary of Bernard, *Vetus,* p. 175.

11. Jean Mabillon, AA SS OSB, vol. IX, Preface, #11. pp. lxj-lviij. Paris, 1701. See also, AA SS OSB, vol. III, Preface, #1, 20, 21, 22, pp. x-xiv. Paris, 1672.

12. 'Woher Kommen die Laienbrüder?' *Analecta Sacri Ordinis Cisterciensis.* 12 (1956) 1-104.

13. See Giles Constable, '"*Famuli*" and "*Conversi*" at Cluny. A Note on Statute 24 of Peter the Venerable,' *Revue Bénédictine.* 83 (1973) 326-350, and the article by Wolfgang Teske, 'Laien, Laienmönche und Laienbrüder in der Abtei Cluny. Ein Beitrag zum "Konversen-Problem" I Teil.' *Frühmittelalterliche Studien* 10 (1976) 248-322.

14. *Statuta Petri Venerabilis,* edited by Giles Constable. *Corpus Consuetudinum Monasticarum.* t. VI. p. 74. Siegburg, 1975.

15. 'Statuts d'Hugues V, Abbé du Cluny,' *Statuts, Chapitres Généraux et Visites de l'Ordre de Cluny,* t. I, p. 42. edited by G. Charvin. Paris, 1965.

16. 'Statuts de Bertrand Ier, Abbé de Cluny,' *Statuts, Chapitres Généraux* I, p. 89.

THOMAS BECKET AND MONKS' BREAD

Lawrence C. Braceland, S.J.

Gilbert of Hoyland and Serlo of Wilton are authentic cistercian voices of the twelfth century. In transcribing and translating passages from manuscripts in The Bodleian Library, Oxford: Bodley 87, Trinity College 19, and Rawlinson G 38, I originally failed to distinguish between these two great imaginations in the service of affective theology. Elsewhere I shall present the evidence for Gilbert's authorship of a prologue and two sermons on Matthew in Bodley 87, ff. 89v-98v; here I wish to highlight as a literary and historic event the survival in this manuscript of two passages of Master Gilbert, abbot, concerning 'our famous protomartyr,' who can be none other than Thomas Becket. In the second part of this paper I shall present Master Serlo of Wilton as the author of a commentary on the Our Father, found both in Trinity College ms. 19 and Rawlinson ms. G 38; here I shall present a translation only of the fourth petition of the Our Father, in which Serlo's imagination also soars in the service of affective theology.

Thomas Becket

Before the presentation of two passages from Gilbert on Thomas Becket, it will be helpful to review the calendar of pertinent events of 1170-72:

1 Dec. 1170: Thomas Becket's final joyful return to Canterbury;
29 Dec. 1170: eight days after his fifty-second birthday, at dusk on a Tuesday, Thomas' murder by the sword at Canterbury;
21 Dec. 1171: feast of the Apostle Thomas and birthdate of Thomas Becket, reconciliation of Canterbury Cathedral after its desecration;
26 Dec. 1171: a first, as yet unidentified, sermon on St Stephan, the protomartyr, was delivered as, I believe, part of a triduum of prayer begun in preparation for 29 December, the first anniversary of Thomas' death;
27 Dec. 1171: a second sermon with final passage on Thomas the protomartyr;
28 Dec. 1171: a third sermon with introductory passage on Thomas the protomartyr;
22 May 1172: apostolic absolution of King Henry II, at Avranches;
25 May 1172: death of Gilbert of Hoyland at l'Arrivour.

Final passage in the first extant sermon on our Protomartyr

The text of the two sermons is taken not from the Mass of St
Stephen but from the Mass of the Common of Martyrs outside Paschal-
tide. The body of the sermons is taken from a running commentary
on Matthew 10:34-42, which may be from Gilbert's lost commentary on
Matthew. Inserted at the end of one sermon and at the beginning of
the following sermon are the two passages which mention 'our protomartyr,' though not Thomas Becket by name.

> *Our famous protomartyr, whose feast we joyfully recall
> today, welcomed his cross, followed Jesus. He went out
> 'to him outside the camp, bearing abuse for him' [Heb 13:
> 13]. O lucky man, because 'the reproaches of those who
> reproached you,' good Jesus, 'fell upon' him [Rm 15:3].
> The great saint went out, 'outside the camp' following
> Jesus, 'outside the camp' of his body and 'outside the
> camp' of the city, for his Lord also 'suffered outside
> the gate' [Heb 13:12]. 'Now casting forth the proto-
> martyr, Stephen,' according to Acts, 'they were stoning
> him' [Ac 7:58]. It is a great sign of a protomartyr that
> he has something in common with them, i.e. the Lord and
> Stephen , for he suffered outside the gate with the Lord
> and protomartyr Stephen. Of his own will he laid down
> his soul for his Lord, but see how many souls he had al-
> ready raised up in reward! He gave his own soul and he
> has already welcomed so many souls in exchange for his
> own. 'If he lays down his soul,' says the prophet, 'he
> shall behold a longlived progeny' [Is 53:10]. And you,
> our blessed protomartyr, have laid down your soul in death
> for your Lord. Behold, now you see a longlived progeny,
> countless descendants! 'Lift up your eyes,' holy patron,
> 'lift up your eyes round about and see. All these hosts.
> ...have come in your honour' [Is 60:4]. What remains but
> for you to pray that as many as you wish may come to you,
> for they are coming in your honour. At your intercession,
> those who persevere in following you with praise, may fol-
> low in virtues, no rather may follow the one you followed,
> the Lord Jesus, because he who welcomes the cross and fol-
> lows Jesus, is found worthy of him. Now may the Lord him-
> self be willing to grant us this through your prayers, for
> he lives and reigns with the Father and the holy Spirit,
> God, for ever and ever.*

Here it is not difficult to see 'all these hosts' coming on pilgrimage to Canterbury to honour 'our patron' and 'our protomartyr' who
himself followed 'outside the camp' and 'outside the gate' the proto-

martyrs Stephen and the 'good Jesus,' Gilbert's favorite invocation.

Introductory passage in the Third Sermon on Our Protomartyr

The rubric introducing the next sermon indicates: 'Here likewise begins a sermon on the same martyr prepared by Master Gilbert':

*Today a large and obvious introduction opens for my ser-
mon and the audience is large. The obvious opening is
the keenness of this large audience. But does not this
very solemnity of the martyr, which during these days
we are celebrating with ceaseless joyfulness, also offer
us an occasion to speak and to unbar the entrances of
our sermon? Indeed I notice your alacrity in praising
the saint. Now I take for granted the increasing importance of the saint, if the breath of a moderate ex-
hortation comes to enkindle the flame of your own keenness. Now would that we might be as keen to emulate
the saint as we are to praise him. If emulation is difficult, [f. 95r] because of the suffering of his death,
still 'love is as strong as death' [Sg 8:6]. Is it not
really stronger? The fervor of love is more passionate
than the horror of death and death is robbed of its power to terrify, when 'perfect love drives us on' [2 Co 5:14].
Our famous martyr did not fear death but by the sword he
passed over into joy. In the book of Job we read that
'they will perish by the sword and be consummated in fol-
ly' [Jb 15:13]. But our saint perished by the sword and
was consummated in glory. Why should he not be consummated in glory, who was consummated in justice? Consummate
love is consummate justice: 'No one has greater love than
to lay down one's life for one's friends' [Jo 15:13]. This
is consummate justice, this is consummate love, to merit
Christ at the cost of one's life. The martyr's flesh was
consumed by torture as he was consummated in justice. He
did not esteem his life dearer than himself. He did not
esteem it dearer than his God. For Christ he offered his
life to death and was esteemed worthy of Christ.
     You have just heard God saying in the Gospel: 'one
who does not accept his cross and follow me, is not worthy of me' [Mt 10:38]. From this verse we should begin,
because with this verse yesterday we came to an end....*

From the content and particularly from the last sentence above, the
link between the two sermons becomes clear and confirms the unity
of authorship. Here also are many minor touches of Gilbert's style,
the paradox for example: '*per gladium transivit in gloriam*' and the

word-play, *consumpta est martyris caro...et ipse consummatus*.

Monks' Bread

The following passage is taken from a commentary on the *Pater Noster* (ff. 127r, c. 1 -- 128r, c. 1) in Trinity College ms. 19, now in The Bodleian Library. As I transcribed and translated the fourth petition of this commentary, I was hoping it would prove to be part of Gilbert's commentary on Matthew mentioned above. I could not but think of the generations of monastic bakers who ruminated on the Lord's petition: 'Give us this day our daily bread.' I re-called Brother Maurus of O. L. of the Prairies and all the monks at Genesee with their recipe for Monks' Bread.

I wondered at the author's creative imagination in linking texts. The Lord is the bread 'who came down from heaven,' of course, but true to the trinitarian theme running throughout this commentary, in the fourth petition the author sees the Lord as a loaf of one of three kinds suitable to the days of our **pilgrimage**. The first loaf is *panis subcinericius*, bread baked under ashes, the God-MAN where the visible emphasis is on the historical man. The second loaf ˙is *panis reversatus*, bread turned around, the man-GOD, where the emphasis is on God in man's body during the **forty** days between the Lord's Resurrection and Ascension. These first two terms are found in Isidore's *Etymologiarum sive Originum Libri*, book XX, ii, 15, on *panis, subcinericius, cinere coctus et reversatus: ipse est et fo-cacius*. The third loaf is called *superius inferius*, the upside-down loaf, the bread which is the glorified Christ, the food of those who with delight contemplate and marvel at the Godhead, the food for the third day when Christ shall have 'restored the kingdom to his God and Father, in the double stole of his body and soul':

> *'Give us this day our daily bread'* Mt 6:11 . *Lord Jesus, provide us with three loaves in your triduum, for you said: 'Today and tomorrow I toil and on the third day I finish my course'* Lk 13:22 . *The first day is life in the flesh, as long as the body is quickened by the soul. The second is life of the spirit, which the soul lives without the body. The third will be life in the double robe of body and soul, when Christ shall have restored his kingdom to God and his Father. Lord, give us this day the* **loaf** *sufficient for every day, 'the bread which comes down from heaven'* Jo 6:33, *yourself the Bread, good Jesus, for nothing is sweeter to the taste, nothing healthier for the hungry.*
> *Yes, in three ways you feed your own with yourself, as with three kinds of bread. The first bread, which we may call the God-man is a loaf baked under ashes, the*

firmest bread indeed for your people, but for your enemy
'the sword of the Lord and of Gideon' [Jg 6:20, 7:20].
What is God if not life and bread and what is man if not
dust and ashes? And what is man, with God hiding and man
visible in one person, if not a loaf baked under ashes,
as if the loaf were God hidden and man manifest? Let
this loaf be reversed, so that the ashes be hidden and
the food be in the open; then he will be a living loaf,
that he may be called the man-God. In the former loaf
the **bread** supports the ashes as if it were pitifully passing into corruption; in the second loaf the bread con-
ceals the ashes as if wonderfully bypassing corruption.
Hence it is that the Lord, in his suffering and obvious
humanity, preached to the world his hidden divinity.
But after his resurrection, to those who had no hesita-
tion about his divinity and thought they saw him in person, by touching and by dining and by many proofs he
proved himself a true but hidden man.

        Therefore the first bread is a loaf baked under ashes,
the God-man; the second is a loaf reversed, the man-God.
The bread before his death was the loaf baked under ashes,
but **after** his resurrection the bread was the loaf reversed. The third bread is neither a loaf baked under ashes
nor a loaf reversed but an upside-down loaf without ashes,
without a loaf-pan and without bran, made of the finest
wheat and not a mix of this nature and that. This loaf
refreshes all things and never fails. It is ever beautiful and bright, ever fresh and warm, never to be changed
on the Sabbath [Lv 24:5-9], never to be removed for another. But who is this loaf? He is the God-God, the super-
angelic, supercelestial, supersubstantial bread. He is
the God-God not of an enumerator but of a ruminant, for
it does not satisfy piety to invoke God once or a second
time unless one adds 'my' God, for the cry of the devout
is 'O God, my God' [Ps 21:1]. For what will it profit me
to cry 'God,' unless he is 'my' God? Let God effect this
for me and add that he is 'God, my God.' The first bread
is food, therefore, on our pilgrimage of body and soul,
that we may follow the footsteps of God 'in holiness and
righteousness all the days of our life' [Lk 1:75]. The
second food belongs to the soul alone as it says in ex-
pectation: 'O Lord, you have singularly founded me in
hope' [Ps 4:10]. He will indeed reform 'our lowly body
to be like his glorious body' [Ph 3:21]. The third food
belongs to those who with delight contemplate and marvel
at the Godhead. Paul who had a brief foretaste of that
sweetness, remarked: 'Even if we once knew Christ in the

flesh, that is not how we know him now' [2 Co 5:16]

Who authored this commentary on the Our Father?

When first I presented this paper at Kalamazoo in May 1980, I was almost convinced that Gilbert of Hoyland was also the author of the Commentary on the Our Father in ms. Trinity College 19, ff. 127r, c. 1--128r, c. 1. His authorship had been suggested by Fr Jean Leclercq and many of Gilbert's characteristics seemed to emerge in the style. In the last passage cited above, I noted his favorite invocation, 'good Jesus,' his reference to the God not of an enumerator but of a ruminant (see CF 14:85f, CF 29:294, CF 26:547), the three adjectives supereminent, superbeautiful, superworldly (see CF 20:266). Although I abandoned the attempt to reproduce in English the Latin wordplay in the last sentence, still I recognised the author's desire to present a memorable idea in a memorable mnemonic: *cujus dulcorem Paulus paulisper praegustatus ait.*

On my return from **Kalamazoo**, I reviewed the manuscripts and literature. Trinity College ms 19 contains a series of forty-three sermons or excerpts. The first six are attributed in the margin to A.C. who turns out to be St Bernard, Abbot of Clairvaux; the final thirty-four are ascribed to A.R. who turns out to be St Aelred, Abbot of Rievaulx. Of the three **intervening** sermons, the third *Ibimus viam trium dierum,* has no ascription, but the first two, *Pater Noster* and *Seraphim,* are ascribed to A.S., i.e. to *abbas swinesheuedensis,* Gilbert of Hoyland, according to Jean Leclercq in *Mediaeval Studies* 15 (1953) 102-3, or rather to *abbas savigniacensis,* not further identified, according to C. H. Talbot in *Sacris Erudiri* 13 (1962) 153.

Fortunately I remembered a work in ms. Rawlinson G 38, which I had used already, for it begins with the letters, treatises, unfinished sermon and *Mira Simplicitas* of Gilbert of Hoyland; the manuscript continues immediately with a short **introduction** leading into a more polished version of the *Pater Noster* of **Trinity** College 19. This introduction opens with the dedication: *Servis Christi conservus eorum Serlo dominicam orationem,* then cites the text: *Protector noster aspice Deus et respice in faciem Christi tui* (Ps 83:10), continues with this incipit: *Protector noster Deus Pater est...*and this desinit: *Universos docuit Filius naturalis adoptivos semper orare et non deficere dicens* (Lk 18:1), *Pater noster qui es in caelis* (Mt 6:9). Could I be certain that the Serlo of the introduction: *Protector noster,* was also the author of the splendid commentary on the *Pater Noster* which followed?

In the article on *Serlon,* fourth abbot of Savigny, in DTC 4 (1941) c. 1940, J. Mercier said that the commentary on the Our Father, which several manuscripts attribute to this Serlo of Savigny, should be considered the work of the Englishman Serlo of Wilton.

A. S. then turns out to be neither Gilbert of Hoyland, Abbot of
Swineshead, nor an Abbot of Savigny, but Serlo of Wilton, who became abbot of l'Aumône, *de Eleemosyna,* a foundation of Cîteaux.
Little did I know that I had been in search of an old friend, whose
commentary survives in at least twenty manuscripts and whose authorship seems uncontested.[1]

St Paul's College
The University of Manitoba

NOTES

1. See A. C. Friend, 'The Proverbs of Serlo of Wilton,' in *Media-
    eval Studies* 16 (1954) 179-218; F. J. E. Raby, *A History of
    Secular Latin Poetry in the Middle Ages* (Oxford, Clarendon,
    1934) II, 111-115. Morton W. Bloomfield, *et al, Incipits of
    Latin Works on the Virtues and Vices, 110-1150 A.D. Including
    a Section of Incipits of Works on the Pater Noster* (Cambridge,
    Mass., Mediaeval Academy of America, 1979) nos. 8357, 8936,
    9128; here Trinity College 19 seems to be omitted and also
    Leyser 428 which is mentioned in Hauréau, *Incipits,* Appendix
    II, p. 253. I wish to thank the Keeper of Western Manuscripts,
    The Bodleian Library, Oxford, for permission to cite MSS. Rawl.
    G. 39 and Bodley 87, and for permission on behalf of Trinity
    College, Oxford, to cite Trinity College MS 19, deposited in
    The Bodleian Library.

CISTERCIAN PUBLICATIONS INC.

Titles Listing

THE CISTERCIAN FATHERS SERIES

THE CISTERCIAN STUDIES SERIES

EARLY MONASTIC TEXTS

Evagrius Ponticus—Praktikos and
  Chapter on Prayer   CS 4
The Rule of the Master   CS 6
Dorotheos of Gaza—Discourses and
  Sayings   CS 33
Pachomian Koinonia I:
  The Lives   CS 45

CHRISTIAN SPIRITUALITY

The Spirituality of Western Christen-
  dom   CS 30
Russian Mystics
  (Sergius Bolshakoff)   CS 26
In Quest of the Absolute: The Life
  and Works of Jules Monchanin
  (J. G. Weber)   CS 51
The Name of Jesus
  (Irénée Hausherr)   CS 44
Gregory of Nyssa: The Life of Moses
                                        CS 31
Entirely for God: A Life of Cyprian
  Tansi (Elizabeth Isichei)   CS 43

MONASTIC STUDIES

The Abbot in Monastic Tradition
  (Pierre Salmon)   CS 14
Why Monks?
  (François Vandenbroucke) CS 17
Silence in the Rule of St Benedict
  (Ambrose Wathen)   CS 22
One Yet Two: Monastic Tradition
  East and West   CS 29
Community and Abbot in the Rule
  of St Benedict I
  (Adalbert de Vogüé)   CS 5/1
Consider Your Call
  (Daniel Rees)   CS 20
Households of God
  (David Parry)   CS 39
The Rule of Iosif of
  Volokolamsk   CS 36

CISTERCIAN STUDIES

The Cistercian Spirit
  (M. Basil Pennington, ed.)   CS 3
The Eleventh-Century Background of
  Cîteaux
  (Bede K. Lackner)   CS 8
Contemplative Community
  (M. Basil Pennington, ed.)   CS 21
Cistercian Sign Language
  (Robert Barakat)   CS 11
Saint Bernard of Clairvaux: Essays
  Commemorating the Eighth Cen-
  tenary of his Canonization
                                        CS 28
William of St. Thierry: The Man &
  His Work
  (J. M. Déchanet)   CS 10

The Monastic Theology of Aelred
  of Rievaulx
  (Amédée Hallier)   CS 2
Christ the Way: The Christology of
  Guerric of Igny
  (John Morson)   CS 25
The Golden Chain: The Theological
  Anthropology of Isaac of Stella
  (Bernard McGinn)   CS 15
Studies in Medieval Cistercian
  History I   CS 13
Studies in Medieval Cistercian
  History II   CS 24
Cistercian Ideals and Reality
  (Studies III)   CS 60
Simplicity and Ordinariness
  (Studies IV)   CS 61
The Chimaera of His Age: Studies on
  St Bernard (Studies V)   CS 35
Cistercians in the Late Middle Ages
  (Studies VI)   CS 38

STUDIES BY DOM JEAN LECLERCQ

Bernard of Clairvaux and the Cister-
  cian Spirit   CS 16
Aspects of Monasticism   CS 7
The Contemplative Life   CS 19
Bernard of Clairvaux: Studies Pre-
  sented to Jean Leclercq   CS 23

THOMAS MERTON

Thomas Merton on St Bernard
                                        CS 9
The Climate of Monastic Prayer CS 1
Thomas Merton's Shared Contempla-
  tion: A Protestant Perspective
  (Daniel J. Adams)   CS 62
Solitude in the Writings of Thomas
  Merton (Richard Cashen)   CS 40

FAIRACRES PRESS, OXFORD

The Wisdom of the Desert Fathers
The Letters of St Antony the Great
The Letters of Ammonas, Successor
  of St Antony
The Influence of St Bernard
Solitude and Communion
A Study of Wisdom

*   out of print